Xin Publishing

Heero Miketta...

born 1973, Karate since 1989, holds several black belts in different Karate styles. During his time as a professional teacher he founded four dojos and initiated the ShoShin Projekt. He also works as a trainer for communications in companies and is a founding member of Prävent e.V., an organization for violence prevention, founded by the police in Bergisch Gladbach, a German city close to Cologne. Today he mainly works as a writer.

Patrick Ehrmann...

born 1985, started his Karate training 1991 in one of Heero's children's groups. Today he works as a professional teacher of Karate in his own dojos. He also is a lecturer for the German Karate foundation KDNW e.V., where he is responsible for training with children and adolescents. His wide range of education includes traditional Karate-Do and self-defence as well as modern forms of training like Kara-T-Robic or Sound-Karate. As an expert for outdoor training he brings great diversity to any of his lessons.

The ShoShin Projekt...

... is a network of German martial arts teachers who are keeping "beginner's spirit" in their work, themselves aiming to continue learning. In martial arts like in any other part of life many experts regard their own development as complete - but whoever wants to develop further needs an open mind and the ability to be amazed and accept new impulses.

"In the beginner's mind there are many possibilities,
in the expert's very few."
Shunryu Suzuki

http://www.shoshin.info

Heero Miketta ♦ Patrick Ehrmann

Bonsai Martial Arts

Kid´s Karate
Kid´s Ju Jitsu
Kid´s Kickboxing
Kid´s Kung Fu

A proven concept for
martial arts training with children

Published by Xin Publishing
an imprint of Xin He Ltd.
Suite 404, 324 Regent Street
London, W1B 3HH, UK

Copyright © 2010 Xin He Ltd.

All rights reserved. No part of this publication can be reproduced, stored in a retrieval system, or transmitted in any form or by any means, electronic, mechanical, photocopying, recording or otherwise, without the prior permission of the publishers and/or authors.

German original: © 2009 Heero Miketta

Translation:
Heero Miketta & Oliver Pfuner
Proofreading:
Lyn Thurman

Title photo:
©iStockphoto.com/Gerville

Photos:
Patrick Ehrmann
Venjin He

ISBN: 978-0-9564897-2-2

Table of Contents

Preface	7
1. Target definition	11
2. Violence prevention and conflict	19
3. The trainer	43
4. Starting a new group	55
5. Rituals and rules	59
6. Techniques and exams	65
7. Background knowledge	81
8. Games	89
Example lessons:	117

Preface

Most martial arts teachers start their career training groups of children. One reason for that is the fact that working with kids is not particularly popular. Shaping the contents of martial arts to fit the children's mind is not only hard work but it also gives you less chance to unfold your own capabilities and ideas than would be possible working with a group of highly-motivated teenagers or young seniors.

It wasn't much different for me in the beginning: Kid's groups were one of my first jobs as a Karate teacher. Interestingly, in one of my first groups a young boy named Patrick Ehrmann started his Karate-career.

In the following decade, I founded five Karate dojos and clearly recognized the importance of children's groups for professional martial arts schools: Kids (boys as well as girls) are very interested in the chance to try out fighting and wrestling – while parents feel a high need to give their children more self-confidence and more safety.

The parents expect even more from martial arts lessons. They want their children to be taught assertiveness as well as the ability for considerateness; they ask for discipline as well as inner peace; they want their children to gain co-ordination as well as physical fitness. The requirements for good martial arts training are enormous.

This adds to the difficulty of making kids interested in the highly-complex topics of martial arts. Despite the fact that martial arts are 'cool', they are a difficult road to travel which demands effort, patience and tolerance.

Taking all this into consideration it's not the best environment for junior trainers, without experience, to be left alone. So kid's groups need a sophisticated, child-focussed approach and they need skilled trainers with a well-developed approach that:

- successfully teaches content,
- is a great deal of fun,
- enthuses the kids and
- convinces the parents.

But there is yet another topic that maybe important for a really successful group: Many times working with children is a job done by (young) women. This is a pity, since most children already are surrounded by females most of the time. At home, in kindergarten or at primary school men are underrepresented.

初心

For this reason I am very happy to work with Patrick developing the Bonsai concept as well as writing this book: He is not only an excellent Karate teacher but also an enthusiastic kid's trainer.

Over the past few years we have developed the ShoShin Bonsai martial arts concept. Numerous children, beginning from the age of 5, took part in our experiments and we can proudly state that nobody got harmed in the process - neither trainers nor trainees!

But we do not only work with kids. The ShoShin Project in Germany offers official licensing workshops for the 'Bonsai Martial Arts Trainer'. These are highlights on our calendars and we always look forward to them very much.

One great thing about them is the playful approach. Games are fun not only for children but adults love them too – even if they sometimes don't admit it. Not only is the list of games also suitable for training with grown-ups – there are many hints and ideas that may very well work for senior's groups too.

Have fun reading and have success using this book!

Heero Miketta
Helsinki, May 2009

初心

初心

初心

1. Target definition

Experience has shown that even in successful martial arts schools there are often no clear schemes or no real concept for children's training.

Many times the first hurdle is the focus of the dojo in general: Martial arts? Sport? Is the training in general fitness-oriented? Does it have a competitive focus? Or is self-defence the main target?

If kid's groups are important for competitive achievements like winning tournaments and trophies then the entire planning has to be shaped towards that goal. In this case the trainers will have to look out for talented students and can not spend time working with less promising athletes. A high rate of repetition is needed; techniques and certain strategies have to be ground-in.

From our point of view this is such a pity, since martial arts are so much more than just sports. Our work is an interface between many important social-cultural issues: It is about social interaction, responsibility, trust and respect, team-spirit, ego-strengthening, the acceptance of other people's limits as well as defending our own, and last but not least martial arts teach how to deal with violence and aggression.

Beyond fitness performance and competitions, we also help kids to connect body and mind. We are all losing contact with our bodies in everyday life. It seems to be a simple requirement of schools to coordinative abilities, but it gains more and more importance in a society that sits down most of the time instead of moving. We will go into detail in the chapter 'violence prevention'.

The ShoShin Bonsai concept focuses on a holistic approach. This provides for a sustained commitment of the children to martial arts, allows for interesting and diversified training and gives the opportunity to really reach kids on a level they understand.

Children are more than just 'small grown-ups'; they are different in their levels of perception and concentration but also in their ideas of what they want to find in martial arts.

Goals from the children's perspective

For children sport in general is a way of finding inner balance and also a doorway to important learning, which is most effective by using the body. In our modern world, in school as well as in everyday life, most input comes on a cognitive level. It is expected of us to use the rational part of the mind to receive information, discipline and focus.

In fact, nobody learns a lot this way. Only a small part of learning happens with the mind. Not only children but adults too make decisions in a large part based on emotions – and emotional learning is done best by physical, practical experience.

<u>Movement</u>

Kids expect real physical experiences with fun, movement, excitement and the possibility to exert themselves from not only martial arts but from sports in general.

They also expect a 'successful experience'. This differs from many grown-ups who may even be spurred on by negative feedback. Children want positive messages.

The second part of the 'successful experience' is the most important: While there is nothing wrong about receiving a certificate or doing well in an exam, these things seem to make parents and grandparents happier than the kids themselves. It is extrinsic motivation, which

means after hard work the result is rewarded by recognition from the outside.

However, more importantly for the motivation of children it is intrinsic motivation, fun and excitement of the everyday training which moves them. The experience that something really works; that something has been accomplished.

Remember: Kids want to be able *to do something*; they don't necessarily want to *learn* something. Motivation needs to be immediate, much more than with adults (but being honest we have to state that this is a rule not only for children. It's true for each training group).

The exotic Asian 'Cool-Factor'

The 'Cool-Factor' is an undeniable part of Asian martial arts. Jackie Chan, Jet Li and the heroes of many cartoon and anime-series on TV illustrate how incredibly cool it is to be a martial arts master. The TV series 'Buffy the Vampire-Slayer' swept a countless number of young girls into our dojo, explaining their motivation by saying: "That looks so great, I want to do that, too."

Of course all the things that look particularly good in those series are either unrealistic or relentlessly hard to learn: High kicks, jump techniques, magical fireballs and, last but not least, fights against multiple opponents without even suffering a small scratch!

Again: Kids want to *do* that, they don't want to *learn* that. Being a coach it will be a frustrating process to teach jump-kicks to kids, since practicing them is hard and boring work. This leads to a situation where the less talented give up while the easy-learners just celebrate amongst themselves.

To accomplish the 'Cool Factor' you need to be a good trainer. We recommend you make room for athletics and acrobatics, but not to make them the centre of attention. The martial arts, with its Asian background, have so much more to offer than high kicks. There's the Japanese language, Chinese written characters, Asian fairy tales and mythology all carefully dosed with knowledge, authentic rituals and exotic clothing – all of these which can be used to generate a sustainable intrinsic motivation for the trainees.

Idols and role models

Although many trainers will disclaim this fact, maybe being humble, martial arts teachers must emit a certain kind of aura. The 'master'

初心

(sensei, sifu, shidoshi) is more than just a coach. There are further demands pushed by the very hierarchic idea of different-coloured belts.

That is not really a problem. It can be a huge opportunity, as long as the teachers handle these ideas responsibly. 'Respect' (although this is an over used word in our modern western societies) is not a bad thing, since it gives the martial artist a chance to teach just through setting a good example.

Be active in a peer group

It's often underestimated, but yet very, very important, that sport means being in contact with others. It is a happy, exciting, well-organized get-together of people sharing a similar taste. It means meeting buddies and friends.

Many successful dojos take this a step further: They include the parents as well as their children, so whole families are active together. This may go far beyond the actual training time in the gym.

Be able to defend yourself

It's the last item on our list, although it is on top of the list from kids: Self-assertion and self-defence; the feeling of strength and secu-rity. On that note, some brawling or some grappling should be part of every lesson as a foundation to deal with physical hassle. It creates successful experiences, meets expectations and offers excellent approaches to social learning.

Goals from the parents' perspective

Self-assertion and self-defence are high on the agenda of most parents too. "My child should learn how to succeed in escalated conflicts" - this sentence illustrates the wish to give our own daughter or son additional security in a world that seems to be dangerous. It also shows how important it is to parents to reduce their own worries.

Social learning

Actually this requirement also finds its limitations anytime the kid decides to use his or her own newly-developed self-confidence to oppose the opinions of their parents – or by starting a quarrel with grandma for not wanting to be kissed by her during a family meeting.

This is the flip side of the coin: He who learns to fortify himself also has to learn how to respect other people's limits. More importantly it is to recognize these limits, since this is the real problem in most cases.

Some parents formulate really surprising sentences during training: "With you, my son suddenly obeys orders. I hardly recognise him", or: "It's amazing how the kids sit still for five minutes at the beginning of each lesson. They never do that at home", or worse still: "Don't worry about giving my son a hard time, he has to learn discipline."

There's self-assertiveness, self-defence, a strong ego on the one side and on the other there's sub-order and obedience – quite a gamut that has to be covered in martial arts-training.

Additionally, not all parents have the same ideas. Some bring their daughter, so she learns 'to not always give in if someone pressurises'; others bring their son because 'our paediatrician said he will learn how to behave here.'

All these sentences are original quotes from our lessons, illustrating the range of requirements that has to be met by the training team. It will only work using group dynamics as wisely as possible. You will find much more information in the chapter about violence prevention.

Fun for the kids

Fun, of course, is an important issue for parents, too. The lessons are supposed to give their children a good feeling, a positive experi-ence, and at home they should enthusiastically report their latest stories from the dojo.

An important tip for the trainer: Demanding, difficult or unpleasant topics belong at the beginning of the lesson. The end of any training should be positive and cheerful, so the children give sunny feedback to their parents.

Performance

Parents love their children – at least in an ideal case – and of course they see them as stars. A trainer will clearly remember that whenever he or she criticizes a kid, since parents fight like lions for their cubs (especially mothers). But it is even more relevant when it comes to performance.

Usually it's the parents who ask first for the next belt exam, how much time it will take to reach a blackbelt, if there are competitions

their kids could attend. Under the same aspect they like to screen the teacher's ability:

- Which qualification?
- Any certificates?
- Which belt?
- Any championship success?

You don't have to play this game, but you should know how to deal with it professionally.

Measuring performance, receiving awards like diplomas, exams, competitions – all this is important, especially for parents, and it is necessary to take this into account. Nevertheless the demand for an 'achievement show' can also be met with a nice presentation during a town festival, a Christmas party with a show or an internal workshop. All these occasions are good chances to generate nice pictures for the family album.

The kids enjoy showing their skills, too. The preparations of a show are exciting, the presentation itself (no matter what form it takes) is even more thrilling, and of course this has a very good learning curve: Dealing with pressure and high expectations.

In this context one thing is really important. Whenever performance is measured or skills are presented, any feedback should be honest. If something is bad, it's really bad. There's nothing worse for children than knowing they were not good at all – and nevertheless people around pretending it was great. It disavows really good efforts; it is humiliating and ruins the fun.

Goals from the school's perspective

Let's say it straight out: children's groups are the backbone of many (if not the most) martial arts schools. Kids groups finance the championship teams of successful dojos and simultaneously ensure their replenishment with talented and eager athletes. Professional dojos depend on a large number of young people in training to keep their business running.

So this is the target direction: The children's groups should be large, they should have a significant multiplier effect, and they should create student retention. In the best case being strong enough to keep the kids in the dojo during puberty related confusion which so often leads to a break in training or even makes the kids leave the dojo.

An even greater success would be if other family members (siblings or parents) follow the children into the dojo.

The danger that lurks therein is opportunism. In too many dojos the training team tries to fulfil too many wishes and is thus inconsistent concerning the content and organisation of the children's training.

Our advice: Stay consistent and in case of doubt prefer risking a crash instead of giving in too fast. Short-term dissatisfaction can turn into a sustainable long-term success as soon as kids and parents find out that their training is following a well-developed, professional concept.

All that is required is good communication towards the parents – and a reliable agreement in the coaching team.

Content Objectives

This brings us to the crucial point: Didactics. The ShoShin Bonsai concept follows a clear principle:

The younger the child, the more holistic the training.

Specialization, performance orientation and technical training should increase slowly with the age of the participants. At that rate the topics of the Bonsai training are highly diverse; they should generate sustained interest and a long-term retention of children in martial arts.

The Bonsai class trains:
- Physical and sporting basics, general motor skills, coordination and perception.
- Basic knowledge of confrontation and fighting.
- Social skills and team skills.
- Dealing with aggression and conflict.
- Self-confidence, self-assertion, self-strengthening.
- Recognizing and accepting of limits.

The training helps compensate the normal daily routine of the children on a physical level. On that basis performance orientation is the second step:
- Techniques,
- Martial arts style (Karate, Judo, Taekwondo, Ju Jutsu, …),
- Exams and (perhaps) competition skills,
- If necessary: rules and specialised skills for the competition system.

初心

2. Violence prevention and conflict

Many martial artists often talk about 'philosophy', pointing out the traditional roots of their styles. It's fairly interesting that many times those who talk the most hardly include any of these ideas in their actual training. One reason for this obvious contradiction is the fact that it is not really clear what exactly 'martial arts philosophy' means.

Very few coaches really give philosophical lectures in their lessons, and it's probably better that way. Introducing background information into the training in a skillful way requires tact and doing it for children also needs empathy and, of course, a lot of knowledge. Even more so if you want to reach out to the children with that information.

At the same time the embedding of martial arts in Asian ways of thinking and behaviour, the connection of physical training and oriental philosophy provides an enormous advantage over other popular sports. We called that the 'Cool-Factor' in the first chapter, but it's much more than that.

This is our recommendation for teachers: Keep the focus on the word *'martial'* in 'martial arts'. Any wisdom in our styles comes from fighting.

Martial arts and violence prevention

From an Asian point of view fighting is much more than a struggle that generates a winner and a loser. For the Japanese, for example, fighting is a 'DO', a way to knowledge – and that distinguishes Asian martial arts a great deal from European or American systems of fighting sports (like boxing or wrestling) that are built around the idea of winning tournaments.

The path to philosophical expertise needs both the will and the ability to deal with yourself and your relationships to other people around you. It is all about rules of social life and even more so in the way you treat yourself and deal with conflicts the right way. To say it simpler: it is all about finding out how the world works and what your own part is in this system. That also includes the question of conflict management and dealing with aggression, including your *own* aggression.

初心

This makes *violence and aggression* one of the central 'philosophical' topics in studying martial arts. Alongside these issues it's very easy to unfold a variety of questions important in everyday life, about your own principles, preferences and social learning.

And this again is the core of 'violence prevention'. The greatest difficulty about this topic is the fact that violence is one of the biggest taboos in contemporary Western society. There are very strong expectations how you have to feel about violent behaviour – and opinions deviating from the norm might make you at risk of becoming the victim of prejudice and opposition.

Unfortunately this produces a lot of hypocrisy and a variety of 'double messages' that can be very challenging especially to educators, teachers and coaches. Ignoring these facts easily leads to the risk of being seen as untrustworthy.

Martial arts workshops headlined as 'violence is not the solution' are as ridiculous as soldiers going to war with a banner saying 'fighting is not an option.' Of course martial arts training is about using violence and the students learn how to fight. This gives them the power and strength to deal with aggression and violence in a way that is safe and de-escalating.

Self-defense and self-confidence are the first steps on the way to prevent violence, and martial arts offer exactly that. But there are many more things to learn in the dojo:

- skills for communication, not only in conflicts
- mutual respect
- recognizing other people's limits
- defense of one's own limits in an appropriate way

Because martial artists are dealing with fighting, conflict and struggle on a regular basis they learn social skills and respect. Asian traditions with their highly dedicated rituals, a deep sense of respect, introspection and emphasis on one's own personality are very helpful on these topics.

But sometimes they are misunderstood: Asian mentality bears intense differences from many Western views. The focus is set much less on individualism with the roots of Confucianism, Buddhism or Daoism leading to ideas very different from those we are used to in our Judeo-Christian society.

So when we talk about philosophy and martial arts, it can't be a simple adaptation of the Asian perspective. Too many times they don't work in our Western society. Also there are focus shifts happening in

初心

modern Asia, too - in China, as well as in Japan, there is a very strong move towards Western ideas and ideals, which leads to an interesting mixture of perspectives. This is then a challenge to Westerners in martial arts as well.

Back to the topic of violence: Even the martial arts teacher himself should address the issues of aggression and conflict. Only then can he credibly include violence prevention and social learning content in his lessons.

Definition of violence

Yes, there is clear guidance on this issue provided by law. Or rather, more or less clear guidance, considering how peppered with exemptions these laws are when it comes to defining violent behaviour and describing the penalties. This shows how difficult it is to deal with aggression.

Even worse: The existing laws simply don't cover large parts of everyday violence, since they are not extreme enough to be relevant for criminal and civil law.

Unfortunately, it's exactly this everyday violence which is the basis for many forms of violence that *do* lead to criminal consequences. Children who never feel safe and loved in their parents' house or at school, who experience no respect and care, or are even victims of permanent pressure and bullying, will grow up learning that violence is needed to survive – and this determines their whole life. Whoever is beaten regularly as a child will very often act the same way with their own children, simply because this is the learned behaviour and alternatives to such are missing.

So, legal definitions are not our concern. Instead we search for a clear definition: When can behaviour really be called violent? Asking teachers or parents, their focus usually is:

- Beating and hitting
- Kicking
- Biting
- Spitting
- Scraping/scratching
- Stealing
- Blackmailing

This already sounds pretty extreme. Recently the list has been added with:

- Bullying
- Violent robbery
- Teasing

However, when we asked children at primary schools, they have less extreme, but very important issues themselves:

- The alarm clock in the morning.
- Homework.
- I have to sit still during school hours and am not allowed to move.
- Others disturb me during lessons.
- Nobody listens to me because I'm only a child.

Students of secondary schools added more:

- Discrimination - because of gender, nationality, or because I am not in an elite school.
- Annoying remarks - from teachers or classmates.
- Imbecilic rules and "laws" at school.
- Worrying about the future.
- Unemployment.

This list is always open to further additions, but these first hands examples have been collected for many years from work inside schools and with kids of many ages, as a part of the work by Prävent e.V.. This association is a spin-off from the work of the Commissioner of Crime Prevention (Kommissariat Vorbeugung) in Bergisch Gladbach, a city close to Cologne in Germany. Violence prevention, assertiveness, conflict-training are the main topics.

What do we learn from these examples?

Obviously violence doesn't start when a fist hits the face - even if this seems to be the idea of at least many adults. Educators, parents, teachers have a huge tendency to equate violence with physical force. This in fact is a very dangerous development!

Three forms of violence?

Common definitions, for example in teacher's training, mention three different kinds of violence:

Physical violence:

This form of violence attracts attention and is usually sanctioned very clearly and straight.

Psychological violence:

Teasing, bullying and lack of respect.

Structural Violence:

This is the enforcement of norms and standards. For example those covered by the work of the police when persecuting law-breakers - or the teacher at the school with prevailing rules or awarding grades. We are talking about sanctions.

It is the third form of violence that is most often not realised as being violence at all. 'It has to be that way', 'it's always been like this', 'you cannot call this small thing violence!' Statements like these are really common and are heard time and again.

At the same time people who drive too fast complain about the sanctions of police officers and feel treated very badly. They see paying taxes as a heavy restriction on their perceived quality of life.

And of course, it's always the teacher's fault when kids receive bad marks at school – an opinion that is usually openly mentioned in front of the kids at the dinner table.

Contradicting messages and bizarre situations

The results are awkward contradicting messages. On one hand, we tell our children: 'You shall not use force. Don't be violent.' Then on the other hand, we ourselves force them to clean up their room, do their homework or sit still every morning at school. All of this being really important and useful, but still witnessed by the "victims" as force, or as violence, used against them.

Thus sometimes bizarre situations emerge: The teachers of a primary school, for example, wondered about a boy who "suddenly" became violent and started beating up a classmate, although he usually 'is such a nice child, never aggressive'.

Taking a deeper look, it became clear: The boy had received a bad grade that very day. At home, pressure was to be expected. This situation led him into the self-perception of being a victim, his aggression, directed against his schoolmates, was just a way out of this notion.

Children and young adults often find themselves in heteronymous positions, where grown-ups demand activities, set limits or judge behaviour. This is often perceived as unfair, and even worse: it makes them feel helpless, as kids usually have no chance to oppose what adults demand of them.

This feeling gets even worse when young people actually *know* they are wrong, but have maneuvered themselves in a stubborn dead-end street.

In this example the teachers were absolutely not aware that a bad grade might victimize their student, and they simply forgot that victims sometimes tend to 'fight back'. The boy was left alone with his aggression, and that is very dangerous. Aggression often arises from inferiority feelings.

Contradicting messages are anything but uncommon whenever it comes to prevention of violence. Most children know the phrase "Don't use swear words" – and yet the best way to learn to swear is sitting on the backseat in the family car when being driven on the motorway. Another great source of bad language for kids is listening to their parents' opinion on certain politicians.

We therefore recommend repealing the three-part definition, since it doesn't really cover the multiple variations of real violence and especially as it leaves out all the many subtle forms, such as teasing and bullying. So this is our definition:

There is no physical violence.

There is no structural violence.

Real violence is always psychological.

It hurts the soul.

We call it psychological violence whenever somebody is hurt. Not physically – since injuries of the body heal fast most of the time and can be forgotten – but mentally or emotionally. Injuries of the soul heal slower and may leave scars for the rest of the life.

It's violence whenever someone is (emotionally) hurt.

Don't stop reading – we are not advocating a world of super-peaceful, always understanding, highly politically correct people. Instead we are re-focusing to a very straightforward definition of violence that leads to an easy approach to deal with aggression and conflict in a positive and efficient way.

It's important to be aware that it is a violent situation whenever a human being is injured, ignored, disrespected, pushed in a corner, set under pressure or threatened by physical or psychological superiority. Physical injuries are, most of the time, just the last step on a long road.

This means that violence prevention is best done with a violence definition that is not operational ('what happened?'), but from the perspective of the victim ('what happened to you?').

This shift of perspective towards a highly subjective approach generates a very simple definition: If someone *feels* violently treated, it *is* violence.

So if educators want to help their fosterlings in dealing with conflict and aggression, what they really should work on are the following abilities:

Empower people to recognize whenever they are behaving violently, hurting other people or crossing their limits.

But at the same time empower them to deal with attacks and injuries without hypersensitive reactions, act with self-confidence and have the ability to withstand minor challenges.

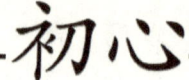

Connected to these two topics is the ability to forgive mistakes and restart relationships even when something went terribly wrong.

What causes violence? A life model

While psychological violence is often hidden and subtle, and therefore harder to see, physical violence is visible immediately, which means it will be sanctioned first.

"Defend yourself with words" is a popular saying among parents and educators. It does not take into account that violence, even if already escalated to a physical level, usually has a long history.

Hardly anyone is able to defend himself using words, fighting back pointedly. The phrase "defend yourself with words" can mean a huge disadvantage to those without high levels of education, to people who have their skills in fields other than eloquence, or more practical and less sophisticated people.

This is one of the reasons why conflicts between people of different educational levels escalate quite often: People who have to stand being goofed at, without a chance of an adequate reaction, may tend to overreact. And, of course, in this case they will shift the conflict to a level that they will certainly win. A verbal discussion between two people – one eloquent and talkative, the other one straightforward but not used to words - may well end up in a fistfight.

Since these examples happen very often, it makes sense to have a closer look at the background of conflicts in general: Where do they come from? What development do they usually take?

There is no lack of complicated explanations and complex models. They usually lead to more confusion and less alternatives of action. So making things more difficult can surely not be the right way for successful violence prevention. The Karate teacher (just like any other teacher or educator, and even parents) needs a simple, straightforward model.

<u>Differing opinions...</u>

... are, first of all, with no conflict, although from time to time in our modern world people seem to believe that. Two people can discuss with each other, even controversial topics, without starting a real quarrel. Discussion might lead to a compromise or even accommo-dation on one side. This works pretty well – as long as both sides feel 'O.K.'; that is: respected, fully accepted and treated decently.

As soon as one side delivers the message that the other one is stupid, inferior, less worthy or simply 'not O.K.', the relationship gets out of balance. It doesn't matter if this message is given on purpose or unconsciously, it mostly leads to a spiral of violence that easily escalates, becoming worse with any new step, as shown in this illustration:

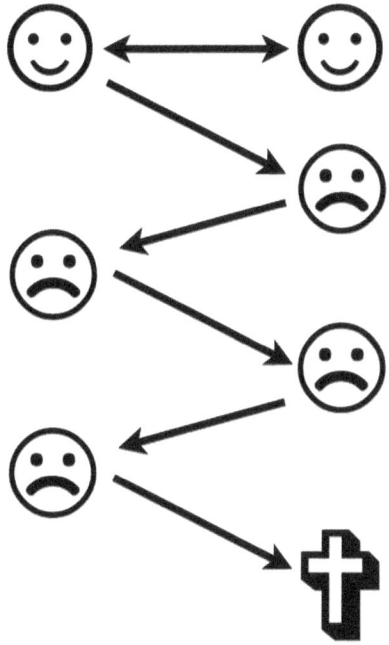

Lack of respect

… instantly unbalances any relationship. When one suddenly feels no longer 'O.K.', it's the best starting point for escalating conflict. Following the definition of violence we introduced before ('whatever hurts emotionally'), the first kind of attack begins here.

Resistance

Those who are not treated fairly, who are disrespected, ignored or suppressed (or at least feel that way) usually react in either of two ways: By withdrawing, retreating, feeling defeated and with the knowledge of being the underdog. Or they start fighting back, of course being completely convinced that this is appropriate, since they are just using their right of self-defense.

This reaction might be totally inadequate, especially in those cases when the resistance follows suddenly after a long phase of withdrawal. Even worse: The 'self-defense' might target people who are not really responsible for the 'underdog-situation', but just in the wrong place at the wrong time.

People who are feeling 'not O.K.' tend to give this state to others; they drag other people into their aura of being 'not O.K.', too.

This can be especially precarious, for example:

Sometimes the culprit, the one who caused the bad feelings, is a situation or a series of events such as the combination of failure at school and pressure coming in from many different sides. In other cases the culprit isn't available for revenge, such as the teacher who gave a bad grade or a police officer who issued a speeding ticket.

This very often leads to a shift of aggression towards other people who actually *are* in reach, although they had nothing to do with the problem itself – like in the case of the pupil who 'suddenly and unexpectedly' became violent against classmates.

Examples

Working with youngsters from the extreme right wing of the political spectrum, claiming to be nationalist or even social nationalist (which, of course, is a big topic in Germany all the time), we find ourselves surprised to learn that none of their violence is really politically motivated. No matter how hard we worked on educating them politically, no matter how clearly they seemed to understand the evil character of national socialist philosophy, the stupidity of their slogans and watchwords didn't really vanish.

That is because those young people don't really care about the politics. They do care about their own ideas of being underprivileged and disadvantaged – and that may even be true for many of them.

Their reaction follows the route we've already described:
- Together we are strong.
- The peer-group we gives us mutual support.
- If we are 'not O.K.' then let's find somebody else who is even less 'O.K.', and if necessary, we can help them to end up in that situation by putting them actively down. Relative to them

we will feel much better off afterwards.
- It doesn't matter who serves as a victim – maybe foreigners, coloured people, homosexuals, women – as long was we have someone to show that we are stronger and superior.

How much this type of violence relates only to dominance and power or how much it is utilized as a compensation for (true or believed) suffered defeats, becomes very obvious as soon as you look at the way people like that treat each other. No matter if they are of 'white power'-right-wing-activists or ethnical gang-members, it's easy to get into trouble with them, even when you belong to their group yourself.

The whole area of sexual violence belongs to the same category: A sex offender hardly ever searches for sex or satisfaction. He longs for power, domination, the experience of strength and violence. He simply looks for an easy victim, someone to reduce to nothing, to remain stronger himself in comparison. This is obviously the reason for child abuse, too – regardless of what the criminals or media may blame on 'sex drive' or 'non-resistible instincts'.

Personality-strengthening

This leads to another issue, since it shows how dangerous it can be to warn children about sex-offenders in a way like 'be careful!'. It is a statement most likely to raise fear – and kids who are anxious are not developing strength and self-confidence. But it's these two things that prevent people from becoming a victim.

Much more importantly than a warning is,

- strengthen children,
- provide them with an idea of what is 'right' and 'wrong',
- clarify that they do have rights and are absolutely allowed to defend them,
- let them know they should listen to their own feelings and learn to rely on them.

A strong, self-confident, communicative, conflict-skilled child will realize if someone does wrong to him; if something is an offense that is not good for the child but only for the offender. She or he will also mention if it is in a relationship that has a 'top and below'-character, generating domination rather than win-win-situations. A well-prepared kid like this will also be able to articulate these facts straightforwardly, thus absolutely not being an easy victim.

初心

This means that strengthening of the individual personality is one of the most important tasks of violence prevention. Doing so, it's important to keep a strong focus on empathy and social skills, so a stronger ego doesn't lead to egoism and recklessness towards others. Self-confidence always needs a strong awareness for others and respect for their boundaries.

To make this work, children (as well as adults) need a solid approach on how to deal with personal mistakes – for their own as well as for those made by others.

Three kinds of mistakes

Dealing with imbalanced relationships means opening up ways to find a new balance. If we assume it doesn't make sense to give in all the time, always obeying other people's wishes, then we need an idea when to forgive others, even when they did something wrong to us and we had to defend ourselves. We recommend introducing three categories:

- *Mistakes we can simply forgive.*
  This includes all those little quirks people have. Somebody is always late for appointments, another one is nervous or hyperactive, perhaps someone talks too fast or likes making mean little remarks, etc. It's easy to ignore minor things like that, as long as the other one is likable in general. Nobody is perfect.
- *Mistakes we can forgive as soon as the other one starts improving himself.*
  These are all those things that need an apology to go along with it. Saying sorry implies the responsibility to do better in the future, to not repeat the same error and to learn. This makes a good basis for forgiving and forgetting: If a mistake is admitted and will not happen again, it doesn't make sense to be stuck with it. It's also important for the way we treat ourselves: Whatever we did wrong, and however encumbering it was, once we recognized and repaired the problem, we should be relieved, knowing that everything is fine.
- *Unforgivable mistakes.*
  There are not many. It's those rare cases when we decide to shut someone out from our life, to never again let him around us. It's also the situation when we decide that self-defense is necessary, whatever it may cost and however hard it will hurt the opponent. A moment of no compromise, no regard. If we have a closer look, we will see that this hardly ever happens.

By separating mistakes into these three groups it helps to see them from a different perspective. Actually there is hardly any misdeed that would lead to a category number three but to be aware of this helps to keep calm, even when anger takes. It's a great help during training, but also in everyday life.

Intermediate conclusion

Of course this model is a very simplified description of highly complex psychological processes. The background of violence is very often highly complicated. But one thing stays the same every time: there is always an imbalanced personal relationship at the beginning, and it's always about the mental state of humans who feel bad compared to others and want compensation.

The same rules apply to everyday conflicts in the schoolyards, for discussions between parents and children, boss and employee, police and citizen. The basic structure of conflicts stays the same – giving us the opportunity to work with a sustainable and reliable definition of violence that helps us understand, analyse and solve quarrels.

Violence prevention has to help people:

- to recognize imbalanced relationships – at best, long before the conflict ends up escalating.
- to notice and respect the boundaries and limits of their own self as well as of others,
- to stand ground in conflicts – but even better to find ways to de-escalate and return to a balanced relationship.

Our definitions make it harder to recognize violence as not every physical punch is violent behaviour and yet other acts which were never previously mentioned, nor apparent at first sight, suddenly fall into the violence category.

Everyone surely has to find their own way to deal with conflict and aggression during his or her lifetime. The martial arts are a very good training ground for these experiences. One important source of individual variation is the difference between men and women – respectively boys and girls.

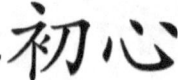

Violence – typical for males?

This statement is heard repeatedly, especially in educational surroundings, and it seems to be reinforced by the apparent fact that males are over-represented in crime statistics.

The problem seems to occur during childhood:

- Boys direct their aggressions to the outside world and thus are mentioned as 'insolent' or 'violent' very easily.
- Girls on the other hand deal with negative emotions internally, their aggressions are directed inside – at least at first sight.

Of course this is a generalization again, and it doesn't fit all boys nor girls, but it is significantly observed. Good evidence for this: Troubled boys develop into aggressive adolescents who pile up problems and conflicts – while girls with deep problems tend to develop eating disorders like anorexia or self-harm behaviour (SHB).

From earliest childhood men and women use very different ways for their 'body communication'. While it is common for girls to hug each other, sit on each other's lap or even cuddle each other, boys have to depend on much harder physical contact with each other.

Brawling and friendly grappling are very masculine ways of showing sympathy for each other. Men prefer harsh greeting rituals and strong language, compared to women.

初心

And yes, this is (again) heavily generalized. In southern Europe for example, men are less distant with each other, rituals are different, but still: Men behave rougher with each other, and scuffling is an important part of male body communication.

The trouble is: This kind of communication is very often prevented when it comes to children in school or kindergarten, because it is misunderstood as a form of violence.

At the same time many female kinds of actual violent behaviour stay unrecognized by educators, teachers or parents because they are less obvious and harder to track: bullying, exclusion, subtle forms of pressure and aggression in peer-groups for example.

For trainers, educators and teachers it's very important to develop sensitivity regarding this issue. But to find this sensitivity can be tricky in everyday life, because it is opposed by one of the worst social developments in our Western cultural circle. We call it de-bodification.

De-bodification and virtualisation

In communication and leadership training, coaching as well as change management processes in companies of all sizes, one thing has been clearly documented over the years: Learning, personal development and also decisions of any kind usually happen on the emotional level of our mind.

People become active most of the time if they believe in something, when they feel that it is the right thing to do, not so much because of rational choice. In most cases reasonable explanations are not the basis for decisions, although they are used to explain decisions (and sometimes to prepare them).

This is especially true in situations where 'rational choice' is supposed to be the background of every activity: In the boardrooms of huge corporations, in politics or whenever it comes to the education of children and adolescents.

A weird mixture? Maybe.

But in all these cases the responsible persons claim to act rationally and completely reasonable – although they follow their intuition to an extreme degree.

However, on which basis are emotions appearing? How do children and adolescents get to know their emotions and feelings, how are they trained to deal with them? And how are adults able to reach their own emotions and use them productively?

初心

The answer lies in the body.

The body is a door to emotional intelligence: Experience, not talking, leads to strong feelings. The body reflects emotions, and vice versa the body influences the world of feelings. The simplest example: Sickness. Even a completely un-harmful cold can change the mood for a long period of time.

Current social developments are not catching up with this truth. Instead, they turn the body into some kind of machine, carrying human beings from one place to the other, but not used actively as the most exciting tool we have to experience the world. In case of malfunction he is repaired, like a car. And just as we take care of a pretty apartment, we make sure our body fulfills a certain level of aesthetics – he has to look good, so we work out, use make up and depilation, cut nails and hair. Throughout life many people change their expectations and switch to a certain quality of looking correct, clean, tidy and well-cared, so they make a 'neat' impression rather than a pretty one.

The more our body vanishes from everyday life, the more people are sitting (in front of the PC, at work, in the sofa watching TV, in a bar or with friends), the less they move and actively collect physical experiences...

... the less they are able to connect to their own self, the more difficult it becomes to reach out for their own feelings, to have a certain 'grounding', a balanced attitude and holistic well-being.

Kids who gather their experiences with (physical) conflicts mainly in front of a computer screen or the TV don't have the chance to improve their ability to react adequately on real conflicts. They are missing the 'restart'-button in real life, they are not used to the pain that is caused by any kind of violence (physical or mental), and they simply are not aware that attacking others causes damage. We often have witnessed how surprised young children are when aggression leads to hurt, especially since this hurting appears on both sides, the loser as well as the winner of a confrontation. Too many children really don't think about the echo they generate from their opponent when they start fighting.

All these important experiences are simply not taught by the virtual worlds of television, computer and internet. Instead, this world just offers strikingly simple truths, very often on a rather primitive level. One terrible example is the vast amount of pornography available on the World Wide Web and easily found by even young children. It is definitely detrimental if these sources are the main part of sexual education, and not parents, educators or even talking with peers.

The increasing de-bodification of our society leads to a virtualization of our life, and this fact aggravates the access to real emotional wisdom.

What does that mean for violence prevention?

The effects of de-bodification and virtualization are counteracting the most important basis for spotting violence and conflict as early as possible and to deal with it accurately: People who are not having a connection to themselves, who are not able to feel their own emotions and deal with it, who do not understand their body and it's messages, are hardly able to develop empathy and kindness for others.

If we stick to the ideas we defined before, violence prevention means helping people,

- to discover imbalanced relationships, early enough to de-escalate conflicts before they ignite,
- to know own self limits as well as mentioning and respecting those of others,
- to stand ground during conflicts – or better: to de-escalate and find a way back to balance the relationship with others if possible.

All this requires great emotional stability as well as high sensitivity which we were talking about before. At this rate the work of sports teachers, trainers and coaches is highly important for social learning and should under no circumstances be considered as just physical education. They work on a major focal point of modern societies. And this especially applies to the martial arts which are strongly connected to social learning by their history and traditions.

For what reason exactly is violence considered 'not okay?

The first response to the question: 'Is violence okay?' usually is: 'No, of course not!'

This attitude is not only politically correct, but also seems to make sense at first sight.

On the other hand it leads to surprising results whenever one of our trainers asks for an example from a group of parents: '*Why* exactly would you call violence not okay? What's wrong with the idea of accomplishing things by using violent force? Why do we want a harmonic and peaceful coexistence?'

———————————— 初心 ————————————

The answers usually come slowly – suggesting that most people didn't really think about this question, but merely adapted a common sense approach that violence is bad instead of really having an opinion. Even worse: Asking for certain examples, many people seem to even *appreciate* violent solutions, ask for stronger punishment of criminals (even for death sentences), want more discipline, more pressure, and so on.

With longer pondering the first answers appear, and they usually follow these lines:

- *Any violence creates an echo.*
  Violent behaviour triggers a spiral of violence (like described above). The obvious solution for the offender is the use of force so massive that there is no chance left for the victim to hit back. This knowledge sometimes further escalates quarrels.
- *Violence will be punished.*
  Among the norms of our society the punishment of violent behaviour is a strong rule. Besides lawful sanctions, violence may also lead to social ostracism in the peer group or beyond. One possible solution for the offender: Don't get caught! (or as an alternative: To argue well enough, so your violence will be accepted socially and not punished by law. This is a method used by many suspects).
- *Violence hurts.*
  ... not only the victim, but also the perpetrator. There is nearly no quarrel that will not lead to at least minor injuries on both sides. This knowledge is extremely important, and it seems that many people who escalate conflicts are not aware of this fact. (a good example for virtualization: You never get hurt while being violent in a computer game.)
- *Using violence as a tool may lead to major losses.*
  A simple truth of escalating conflicts: There will be at least one loser, and there is no guarantee at all who this might be. In most cases it's even worse: When the dust settles down, there will be *two* victims, no matter who started fighting for whatever reason. Therefore, offenders will do all they can to prevent losing the fight. In schools it becomes very obvious: There is hardly any more violence than years ago – but it has become crueler.
- *Violence leads to loneliness.*
  This is not always understandable for kids on first sight, since it seems, that the strongest, the cruelest, the most assertive

guy always has the biggest amount of fans and followers. The catch is that those 'friends' are only loyal as long as the status is maintained. People who have to fight for friends lose them as soon as they lose.
- *Violence causes a guilty conscience.*
  Surely this is the most important thing of all. It's a pity it always seems to appear at the end of a long talk, or that it's not present at all: Who feels for others, who has empathy and an open mind, will feel bad about hurting others. Compassion (not pity!) is a crucial factor for all kinds of violence prevention. Taking responsibility not because it's a duty, but as the desire to establish a close and compassionate emotional relationship to others.

Can violence be 'okay'? And if yes: when?

Let's go back to the question, if violence can be 'okay', if it may be correct under certain circumstances, or at least forgivable. Based on our definition: 'Violence is everything that hurts (mentally)' we face huge problems, since suddenly things turn into violence that could easily be ignored before:

- The ringing of the alarm clock in the morning.
- The enforcement of rules, norms, laws and any agreement about sanctions.
- The awarding of grades.
- Competition for a job.
- The rejection of an unlucky lover.

This makes it even more important to contemplate the 'correctness' of violence.

There are three very important topics:

- self-defense
- Penalties/sanctions/punishment
- Competition

Self-defense

This is by far the most common excuse for violent behaviour. The perpetrator legitimizes his action telling: 'I had to do it, I was defending myself!'

Most teachers have met this argument after sanctioning violent behavior of pupils in the schoolyard – the next day parents would

appear, stating clearly: 'I told my child that he SHOULD show resistance, it's self-defense!'

That's not necessarily wrong: There are, indeed, lots of cases where it's important to clarify one's own boundaries, and depending on the severity of the abuse suffered it may be necessary to emphasize one's own point of view strongly, even by using force.

The lawmakers also share this idea that self-defense is useful and excusable, and thus decided to make it free from sanctions – but only if it can be proved that it was an appropriate response to an actual, present attack.

This is a very good guideline for everyday life, too: Considering the multiple disadvantages that the use of force causes (and the possible collateral damages), no matter if this force is physical or mental, self-defense should be the last resort and has to remain, above all, appropriate. Any overreaction pushes the already high price paid for the use of violence even further.

You need a cool head and a balanced mind to respond appropriately to an aggressive offense. This needs:

- experience in dealing with aggression and violence – even with self aggression and one's own will to react violently,
- a confident and relaxed approach to dealing with offenses and pressure, which needs to be trained by searching for

experiences that deliver exactly these feelings – physical experiences (for example during sports) are most efficient,
- a good intuition for others around us: What did my 'opponent' really mean by his attack? Do I really understand his meaning, or am I the victim of over-interpretation or wrong assumptions?
- the ability to take stick without being whiney – people who interpret the slightest offense as being a massive attack are likely to have huge problems with appropriate reactions.

All this illustrates clearly the importance of sports and physical experiences and clarifies the huge role of sports teachers in social learning.

Penalties and sanctions

Those who are responsible for the sanctioning of rule violations usually tend to rationalize their own violence:

1. It has to be that way.
2. There's no other chance.
3. It's 'only' structural force, not real violence.

These groups include not only police officers or other members of the state executive, but also teachers or managers in companies – it is their job to enforce rules and interests of the community they are working for, whether this is a school, a company or the state. In many of cases this enforcement also has an educational background.

Now that's important: Penalties do have an educational effect! Whatever is not prohibited is surely allowed, and thus it's of heavy importance to clarify boundaries and communicate them straightforwardly.

The problem: Arguing based on 'it has to be that way' very often leads to ignorance for the feelings of the 'victim' of a penalty. Whoever is sanctioned strongly experiences this as a violent offense, no matter whether it's lawful and fair or not.

Students who receive a bad grade are unlikely to point the finger at themselves (as it is expected by teachers and parents), but rather at other people: The teacher was not good at explaining the stuff, the surroundings were too noisy, the others also have bad grades, the teacher doesn't like the student, it's all just bullying, it's unfair. The same applies to traffic offenders: Driving too fast and being stopped by the police they hardly say: 'I am grateful for the information that I was too fast and will show better behavior in future', but start discussing and claiming an unfair punishment. Even a murderer is not happy about the good work of the officers arresting him.

'Violence is whatever hurts (mentally)', which means: Penalties and sanctions are a massive form of violence. They may be right, sense-making, appropriate, and inevitable – but they still trigger a spiral of violence, if they are not already one of many steps of a spiral that started long ago.

In many cases the 'offender' (the one who sanctions) is far out of reach for the 'victim' (the one who is punished): Teachers, parents, police officers. The echo of the violence will not hit the 'culprit' but somebody who has most likely nothing to do with it.

Simple example: The student with the bad grade who has to expect additional high pressure at home will be caught in a schoolyard brawl or a fight on the bus much more easily than another student who received a good grade and looks forward to a happy afternoon.

What do we learn from that?

Sanctions should never come alone. They are a strong message: 'You made a mistake and it is not appreciated'. But they don't help to do better in the future; just the opposite: They generate a loser-position which makes things worse. What is really needed is a plan for learning and action, useful hints on how to develop a more appreciated behavior for tomorrow, after failing in the past. It should describe a way back to be 'okay' again.

Telling people that they did wrong, but not helping them to do better, will support even worse behavior.

(This also applies to positive sanctions: Praise raises pressure, it should come with support to keep up the good work and maintain the newly found status.)

Competition

The third area of violence that is widely accepted in our society, but usually well-disguised, is competition. Any attempt of alternative models of society failed tragically in the past, since competition and rivalry are general human motivations.

Even if people don't want to share this opinion, they still have to admit it: Our actual form of economy and society is competition-driven, and whoever wants to survive in the modern world should be fit to deal with it.

Simplest example: Meat-eating.

There is simply no way to consume meat without killing an animal. Our society virtualized this fact away from public awareness by selling beef not straight from the cow, but from the fridge, nicely packaged in a clean and hygienic box, with a print of smiling animals on the outside.

It's a fairly clear twist of reality, showing how we are less and less capable to deal with everyday violence – like slaughtering animals cruelly just to have a tasty meal on the table.

But competition is an everyday business for everybody, no matter if it is about finding a good job or establishing your own business, being successful by marrying the woman you love or moving into the apartment you want. There will always be others who want what you have, and you will most of the time find yourself wanting something others have.

To win and to lose with dignity (both!) is an ability needed for everyone, so small things like a good friend's bigger car or a neighbour's more beautiful balcony do not challenge one's self-esteem.

Violence prevention also means: Teaching kids to win and to lose, respecting others as well as one's own role in life, so not every competition situation turns into a personal conflict with victims on both sides.

This training is a vital element of any physical education, not only in martial arts, but these fighting sports are the ideal grounds to raise these topics. To be fair and respect others is a main skill of real warriors – and the basics for that is given during Bonsai training.

初心

3. The trainer

In the first two chapters we drafted a main objective for training with children and pointed out that we prefer a holistic approach with the ShoShin Bonsai Concept, rather than an athletic or competitive one. We believe that the topic of violence and conflict is essential to the martial arts in general, and especially in training kids. By highlighting the responsibility of trainers we raised the expectations even higher than they already are. We did this on purpose since, unlike other sports, martial arts have a special mystique which makes people believe that the teacher is not only good at educating, knowing his didactics and methods, but also an outstanding athlete himself; a model of strength in physique, character and impeccable manners.

Of course, this has to do with the Asian roots of martial arts and the certain status teachers have there. The master-disciple relationship is different in the traditional surroundings of martial arts in Asia (although some of it is merely a good show for gullible Westerners).

Nevertheless, although nobody expects a soccer coach to shoot the goals himself, fighting competence is a crucial requirement of a martial arts teacher, regardless of whether he teaches Karate, Judo, Ju Jutsu, Taekwondo or any Kung Fu-style.

But that's not enough. Just like a primary school teacher has to be much more qualified for working with children than their colleagues in secondary schools, colleges or adult education, the children's trainer needs an extraordinary talent to work with kids and the willingness to really engage with them.

This needs sensitivity and self-confidence. Kids are extremely good at noticing moods. A trainer who is not in a good mental shape may blow up a children's group in no time.

Working with parents

It's not only the children who are challenging for the trainer. It's the parents who are, after all, the deciders if their kids attend training or not. They are also the greatest critics; good or bad. Word of mouth reputation spreads faster than any other form of promotion.

初心

The Bonsai trainer needs social skills to deal with this target group successfully: he or she has to be sensitive, empathic, fair and unambiguous with the children and at the same time meet the parent's as a trusted partner.

This includes establishing clear rules, also for the parents. The right behavior in the gym is of high importance: There is no picnic during training, no shoes for anybody in the room, no interference from the side in the training, no comments from the bench – these are typical examples of clear instructions from the trainer to any visitors.

Conversely, he should give the parents opportunities for questions or feedback and (even more importantly) he should provide thorough and comprehensive information.

Written information for parents is important, and it makes sense to involve them in events and offer appointments where children and parents can do something together. It also generates further contacts.

Selection

A real challenge for any dojo is finding the right people for the trainer jobs. Usually it is the young female trainers who are interested in the Bonsai groups whilst the senior trainers usually try to avoid it.

The training is more complex in preparation, more exhausting in the execution and the target group is very demanding. This needs:

- Nerves of steel.
- Charisma of a natural leader.
- Assertiveness – and at the same time sensitivity and understanding. Having only one of these qualities is simply not enough.
- Willingness to continuously learn.
- A highly motivated team player– Bonsai coaches should not work alone (see below).
- An unbiased approach, even if there are favourites in a group (which usually happens and is nothing bad).

And there is one more thing. As we already mentioned before: Children usually encounter women in their everyday life. In most families the father is far less available than the mother, in kindergarten and primary schools the teachers and educators are usually female, and in secondary schools the focus is on learning, not social interaction which takes away the teacher as a role model in many cases.

Children need men.

The lack of male influence is one reason why it makes sense to find men as coaches in Bonsai groups. Conversely, in continuative groups female coaches are needed much more often than is common today.

All of these requirements do not necessarily qualify Bonsai groups as the right place for the education of junior coaches. In the actual work nevertheless there are some reasons why it could make sense anyway: Working with children trains their educational ability and social skills, and in most cases the training in Bonsai groups is led by a team, not by one single coach.

Besides that, it simply doesn't make sense to ignore the fact that most martial arts teachers start their career in children's groups.

Working as a team

It's difficult to handle children's training all alone, even for an experienced trainer. It would reduce the quality substantially, since one person cannot meet all the individual needs of the children.

The minimum for a well-functioning group is a team of two, better still is three coaches, which also offers the opportunity to involve junior coaches: First it gives them experience, they become a solid role model for the children, and it's great support for the head coach of the group.

A team like this can work really focused: One coach takes care of the content of the lesson, the others provide assistance to the children and also intercept any kind of problem appearing during the lesson. This includes handling noisy and disruptive kids through extensive care; stopping negative interferences and caring for injuries without allowing them to interrupt the lesson or scare the other kids.

Experience shows that it works best with a clear division of labour: One of the trainers is responsible for the ongoing lessons and has written the guidelines for the lesson beforehand, ideally one in a long series of lessons. This concept also covers the responsibilities during the training: Every coach leads a part of the lesson more or less on his own, while at the same time the other coaches are taking care of any side topics that may appear (as mentioned above).

Usually none of these concepts ever stand the reality-test. Every lesson is completely different from the way it was planned, but the concept helps the team to co-operate, guarantees a good start and prevents any kind of helpless "what do we do now?" situation that may appear otherwise.

Dealing with special situations

Even if a lesson concept works according to the plan – one of the following situations may shatter it anyway. An experienced trainer usually handles them very easily, especially if he is not alone in the gym and somebody else can keep the lesson going. But preparation is necessary anyway.

<u>Injuries</u>

The first rule of thumb: Do not allow injuries to get the centre of attention. The injured person may feel that even small injuries are exceptionally awful if everybody in the room supports this perception.

For those not injured, witnessing the situation may generate a "scaremonger". This also applies to any parents watching from the bench. And even the 'culprit', if there is one, will feel much worse the bigger the fuss. It is definitely the job of the co-trainer to treat the injury and care for the victim, while the rest of the lesson continues.

In general, there is no sports-injury that can't be treated with cold clear water. In the worst case a kid has a break and sits on the bench for a while. It's also helpful to raise an injured arm or leg, so the kid may lie down instead of sit. In really bad cases the trainer will not be able to deal with it adequately anyway. Calling the parents or, in the worst instance, an ambulance is obligatory in those cases. (Of course in really bad situations, which hardly ever happen, 'cold clear water' is not an alternative to first aid!)

If somebody is bleeding, a patch or a plaster helps – not only physically, but also mentally, since it gives the feeling of being well-cared for, it takes away the fear and it is something to show off afterwards.

Stay calm! In 99 percent of cases the physical injury is just a minor problem (if one at all). Shock and fear are the real problems to be treated first, even in really bad situations: Only a calm victim can really provide reliable feedback about the severity of an injury.

Act immediately, never hurry and speak calmly and peacefully.

Only in rare, exceptional situations, when somebody else is really responsible for the violation and the injury, can this be addressed with the whole group as an example of behaviour, responsibility and fairness.

Quarrels in the group

We already discussed this issue in the chapter "violence prevention". There are many useful hints for trainers in that chapter. Here are some guides for everyday work:

Sanctions and penalties are well known in many dojos but are not really helpful most of the time. In many cases they are even counterproductive.

Mediation in conflicts is a very difficult task, and identifying the culprit is nearly impossible in most of the cases – especially in the limited time of martial arts lessons.

In any case, the trainer should not get stuck with the question: "Why?"

"Why did you quarrel?" is a question never really answered in an escalated brawl. The result is usually two different stories, the truth is not verifiable, and the question "Why?" even raises the pressure on the opponents to justify themselves.

But there is only a reason to justify yourself if you did something wrong. The one with the better answer is better off, and gives those kids who are verbally talented an advantage – although they might not be free of guilt. The whole situation will raise the idea among the disputants that the trainer wants to sanction them for doing wrong.

It is better to direct any questions towards the future instead of the past. Nobody can change the past, but talking about the future opens the door to better behavior: How should this situation go on? How will you deal with each other tomorrow? What will it take to put an end to the dispute? What do you expect from your counterpart so you can stop being mad at him?

Two things are important:

Clarify the reason why the trainer intervened in the dispute. This is best done in the form of a personal message: "I don't want you to brawl now. I cannot teach if you are disturbing the lesson. I am pretty annoyed you started to quarrel again. How do you think this will continue?"

It's possible that one of the two opponents (most likely both) made some mistake that led to the fight. But hardly any mistake is unforgivable if a seriously intentioned apology was issued, together with a real intention to do better in the future. This is important: A low-voiced, mumbled excuse (a pure formality) is not enough and can not be accepted!

To make it easier for the trainer he should be able to appeal to clearly defined group rules:

- Martial artists do not lose control.
- Martial artists respect each other.
- Martial artists know how to argue fairly, reasonably and find a solution for the future.

It is essential that quarrels are not discussed in front of the whole group but are handled by one of the coaches, while the lesson continues uninterrupted at the same time.

Parents in training

Working as a children's trainer for many years, you will most likely experience the intervention of parents as an annoying disturbance from time to time. On the other hand parents are the most dedicated supporters for any kind of activity, not only during training but also when it comes to extra curricular activities.

In general parents have the right (and the duty) to be concerned about what happens to their children during training. It is better they care too much than if they use the dojo as a "parking lot" where they drop their children and disappear instantly.

But just as mentioned before: Parents are not professionals and they should not intervene in the lesson under any circumstance. And that is also true if they are teachers or educators themselves, or martial arts

experts: If they want to watch the lesson, they are bound to the role of an observer and have to adapt to certain rules:

- Nobody interrupts the lesson.
- Spectators behave quietly; they come and go without noise.
- No picnic: Nobody eats or drinks in the dojo.

Criticism is welcome – after training, in private, in a reasonable tone. Above all it has to be constructive. Parents as well as children attend the training voluntarily. They can leave at any time if they are dissatisfied.

The best case is for parents to watch the training in the beginning, but after a little time leave the group and their child alone. By them not always sitting on the bench, children can develop social skills on their own without the backup of their parents.

To help parents accept these rules, it's important to keep them informed. Right away from the first lesson they should get an information leaflet: "What is Bonsai training?"

It is a good idea to organize events that involve parents as well as their children – for example around Christmas or in examinations.

Authority

Children are the most attentive target group possible. They are highly sensitive and feel any kind of disturbance in an instant. A trainer who doesn't feel well will be able to generate an emotional imbalance of the group in a split second.

To gain authority in the group a trainer needs an appropriate mix of rigour and friendliness. That is quite a challenge: To be respected doesn't mean to be strict all the time, and surely doesn't mean to act too aloof.

Instead it means to be very clear in ones own messages and announcements, and to stick to your course without being stubborn:

- Don't make a statement until you are really sure.
- Think twice about what exactly you really want.
- Stay friendly, but tough about the facts.
- Make understandable announcements and stay consistent.
- Never give in to pressure. Claim constructive criticism, always in private and with politeness.

初心

Most importantly: No dogmatism. Listen first, take time to think it through then make decisions. It's permissible to say: "Thanks for the suggestion, I will think about it and let you know what I've decided."

If people feel that a trainer is shaky, inconsistent and just trying to be friendly, he will lose any authority because he is seen as fickle and unprofessional.

Some general hints:

Raise your voice only in rare occasions. Trying to dominate the noise of the group will put their volume even more up.

Never speak in falsetto, never speak monotonously, but vary the tone.

Make periods of rest so you don't 'over-boil' the group.

It's most helpful to generate alternations in training. For example a sudden change from "fast and loud" to "slow and quiet".

Penalties

This topic is closely connected to authority. Too many coaches rely on penalties to enforce discipline. This is a dangerous path that threatens the personal status of a teacher.

The purpose of sanctions – whether praise or blame – lies in achieving an educational effect. They help to clarify what's right and what's not.

A penalty does exactly that: Clarify that something was wrong, and it will not be tolerated. But this is only the first step since it's not enough to just state something was wrong. It's by far more important to show the right way of doing better.

Everybody who gets punished needs a guide that helps him get back into a positive state, to behave in a way that is accepted and welcomed.

A trainer does a bad job if he only punishes mistakes as he also has to give the opportunity to develop better skills for the future. In the best case, critique is given in a four-eye meeting; only in exceptional situations does it belong in front of the group. However, in reality it's not always possible – which makes it even more important that criticism leads to solutions and better behavior in the future.

Penalties have to be:

- useful
- hands-on and really working
- related to the actual problem, not standardized procedures.

Education vs. therapy

Common problems for any coach are children with serious troubles. Being a good teacher, in a position of trust and representing the dojo as a safe environment, means kids open up sometimes. And the nature of martial arts training makes social troubles obvious. Of course, a really good educator wants to help once he recognizes a problem – and this may lead him to dangerous grounds.

It's a simple truth that martial arts do not provide therapeutical services for which the coach usually is not qualified anyway.

If the family's doctor sends children to attend martial arts lessons, because it might help their attention deficit disorder, this may be a charming idea and even flattering, but it will also be a challenge for the group. If parents say that their kid is too shy or too anxious in general and should learn to be more self-confident this might be something that can be influenced by martial arts lessons. The same applies to kids who are lacking discipline or are too chaotic.

Family difficulties, stress at school, traumatic experiences can't be treated with martial arts. The training may help to deal with it, but that's all – the teacher is an educator, not a therapist.

Anyone who risks becoming active beyond that point may quickly meet their limits and find himself pushed into a role that he never wanted to have and is not really able to fill properly.

Feedback loops

Repetition is a major factor in children's training. It's a challenge to repeat something already known and still deliver something new to keep the attention high.

One way to do so is the active collection of feedback from the group.

"What did you understand?" is a helpful question.

It may seem boring at first sight, but the question kicks off the brain. To give the question to the group and choose someone to answer it ensures the attention of the kids, since it may be anyone in the group who has to provide the feedback.

Repetition also helps to balance intellectual differences within a group: Kids who think fast may be developing a role of the main talker in the group. Repetition is a chance for kids who need to think longer to have their share of talking time.

It is sometimes quite useful to treat a single child with particular intensity. This may mean that an answer to a question is followed up by the trainer giving more details, hints may be given and the process of thinking is supported. This can activate children with low self confidence or kids who are very quiet in general, and it prevents a situation in which solutions always come from the same little group of very clever children.

Compensation of talent and intelligence

Finally, *all* the attendants of our training have a right to learn, not only the extremely talented or intelligent children. Thus every group needs a balance between the "top stars" and the very slow ones. The kids who know a lot and learn fast should not be left far beneath their capabilities. A good trainer aims to support the weak and still challenge the strong.

Within the regular groups it makes sense to use peer-tutoring, giving the really talented a chance to take responsibility for new members of the group or slower learners.

Setting priorities

It easily happens that a coach frustrates children by giving them tasks that are simply too difficult or too easy. At the same time, it's even easier to generate positive learning outcomes if the content is prepared in the right way for children. One important way to do so is to set the right priorities for what really needs to be learned.

For example: The difference between "left" and "right" is easy for children who are eight years or over. Most exams of authentic Chinese or Japanese styles demand this knowledge to gain the next belt.

With children younger than eight years it is most likely a terrible waste of time to deal with this topic. Small children are simply not able to realize the difference between the two directions – or they have to expend enormous effort that could be better used on more important issues.

The coach needs alternative descriptions for directions: "The side of the wall", for example, or: "The side where I am standing now", or: "Peter's side."

In most exercises it's just enough if the children choose their favourite side.

The height of kicks or punches is also a problem for young children: It's easier for them to concentrate on an actual part of the body rather than obey an abstract description like, for example in Karate, where "Chudan" means the middle part of the body and "Jodan" means the upper part.

In general children understand movements rather than directions. A turn to the left is difficult to grasp whereas move one foot to the other then afterwards move it away to the other side is much easier to understand.

There are various examples of this kind of difficulty. The general advice: If something doesn't work at all, change the wording of the description first. The next step is to reflect on the actual learning goal and if it is worth the effort, or whether it can be changed into something easier for a child's mind to grasp.

初心

4. Starting a new group

Any good training needs preparation, especially in an environment as challenging as martial arts. To establish a completely new group needs additional work. As we already mentioned: Children and their parents are quite a difficult target group, so we recommend investing even more preparation time and effort.

Facilities

Bonsai groups work better with plenty of space and an appropriate amount of material. Usually the groups for the youngest kids (aged 5 to 8 years) grow fastest. The children bring their friends, and word of mouth advertising is never more efficient than with young parents.

This shouldn't be a problem if you have the right number of trainers. But the conditions of the room should be able to withstand these demands:

- Lots of space. A small gym will not be enough.
- Lots of material. Boxes, ropes, balls, mats in different variations.
- Heating. Too many training rooms are unbelievably cold during winter. We have experienced the worst circumstances in Germany, where the city councils save money on the heating. It doesn't work for children's training.
- Cleanliness. In Germany it is becoming increasingly difficult to find gyms that are reliably clean unless, of course, you own it yourself.
- Accessibility. It's best when the kids can reach the gym on their own without the need for the parents to drive them.
- Enough time. Squeezed between a women's gymnast group and an amateur football team, with the first always needing more time than they should to leave the room and the last demanding a punctual start makes it very difficult to work.
- Quietness! One-third of a triple gym is too loud, especially if you have a basketball group on the left side and jazzdance on the right side. There is no chance to rescue the Bonsai lesson in this surrounding, no matter how hard you work.

Training times

This is, finally, the good news: The times in the early afternoon are those usually not wanted by other sport teams. Many gyms are quite unused at this time – if they are not in a huge metropolis. After 5 p.m. most parents are more relaxed too – their working time is over, and they can use the Bonsai lesson to go shopping or fulfill other chores that are waiting for them.

Coaches

There is no chance to handle a Bonsai group 'on the fly' or without a certain amount of effort. It needs attention, more than any other training group in a dojo. The importance of dedicated and qualified coaches are discussed in a separate chapter of this book.

The crew for the Bonsai groups should be reliably prepared before the start of the first lesson. Changing any one of the coaches in the first months of the group will cause serious troubles and high fluctuation.

The contents

A good piece of advice is to prepare the first five to ten lessons in great detail then discuss it with the whole training team to avoid mistakes that might otherwise happen in a new team working with absolute beginners. It will go wrong anyway. In most cases even the most well prepared plans turn to waste at the beginning of the lesson. They do help anyway; giving confidence to the coaches, adding ideas and forcing the team to think through their aims in advance.

Usually parents are very sceptical with any new kind of activity. It´s making sense to appear as professional as possible. You will find some sample lessons in the appendix of this book.

Promotion

It does not help if the offer is good, but nobody knows about it. Once the group is started, the well-functioning cliques of young parents usually lead to ongoing promotion. In the meantime you have to create attention yourself.

Flyer/Handout:

Consider creating a handy folder with essential information aimed at the children´s point of view. It can be distributed:

- in the club itself
- at doctor's surgeries
- in nurseries, kindergartens and playgroups
- primary schools
- cafés
- shops that are frequented by parents and children: hairdressers, toy stores, lottery shops

Trial offers:

Primary schools and kindergartens are often happy about some tester training sessions in the morning, but sometimes lessons in the afternoon are also possible.

But be careful! Long-running, regular workshops in these surroundings can be counter-productive, because they tie up the coach involved, the children never really bond with the dojo, and they may jeopardise the groups from the dojo itself.

Small events with press-coverage

Smaller events help you to become well-known in the community – especially when they are covered by the local press. A little list of local newspapers, regional radio stations or websites is of enormous value. If you give them information regulary and in a friendly manner, you will find out they are read far more often than one would expect.

Free sample training

We recommend allowing every newcomer at least 5 hours of trial sessions for free, not urging a fast contract for the children. The safety to try out the new sport without pressure makes it easier for the parents to decide to go with the Bonsai training – and it makes it much easier for them to bring siblings, friends or kids from the neighborhood.

But after a while it's necessary for them to really join the dojo especially for reasons of insurance.

Pricing

Don't be cheap. Under no circumstances.

Of course many things are cheaper for kids than they are for adults – the cinema, the amusement park, the museum. But if you allow this idea into your dojo, the parents will take it for granted that you are generous and just work hard because you are a good person.

Working hard for low money will not reduce the demands for the highest quality and flawless performance – but it will give the parents the feeling that your work is not of high value. You will end up with a lot of discussions about your qualifications and the results of your work. Discussions that you will not have if the Bonsai group is more expensive. . 'Was nix kost, ist nix': This is a German saying describing this effect. A rough translation would be: 'If the price is low, the quality is low' or, as you might say, if you pay peanuts you get monkeys.

And don't forget: Bonsai groups are expensive for the dojo, too. There is always more than one coach, the lessons need more preparation as well as more material, and the responsibility is much higher.

5. Rituals and rules

A familiar discussion for martial arts teachers is the traditional atmosphere of training. Obviously the rituals of the traditional Budo are attracting a lot of attention and also lead to further questions about the spiritual backgrounds.

The same goes for rules in training. Many coaches hear statements like: "I bring my child to you so you teach him discipline", or: "It's so nice that the children are sitting quietly in a row in the beginning, they learn that nowhere else these days."

These sentences are somewhat painful for a committed teacher, since we are not really aiming to teach ancient virtues of strong order and obedience for its own sake. Rituals and rules of martial arts training have a specific background. They are not made for teaching manners to children.

It's very interesting how many adults don't want to bend to these rules themselves, but ask for explanations whenever anything seems to be militaristic or even "humiliating" in their eyes.

Reasonable rituals

The simplest reason for the introduction of rituals in training (and not only martial arts training) is their ability to generate transparency for the participant. It's especially important for kids to know what they can expect. This also helps the coach in his work. It's much easier to retain a disciplined behavior in a group without pressure, if there is a certain set of rituals that are already internalized.

Rituals also create a community. The kids experience everybody in the group following the same rules, and that helps to recognize each other (even outside the dojo), but it also helps to keep the community comfortable and free of conflicts.

A lot of reasons for disputes can be excluded by ritualized behavior. This includes the teacher-student-relationship. If the appropriate interaction is settled in advance, there is no need for reoccuring discussions. The time saved can much better be spent on other issues.

初心

In addition, rituals are a great hook to introduce Asian culture and philosophy in training. The rituals are a strong hint that not the fighting itself, or simply sports, is the main topic of martial arts.

Last but not least, rituals and rules provide a safe haven: The participants (kids as well as grown-ups) know how to behave, how to deal with each other and the trainer, which prevents emotional stress in the group. For example, the question: "what do I do if I have to visit the toilet during training?" is easily answered by a reliable framework of rules: Greet the trainer, tell him your problem, bow shortly, leave the room, come back, bow to the room, greet the trainer, wait until he sees you, join the training again. That's by far simpler than the question: "how the hell do I make myself noticed without being the center of attention? This is embarrassing!"

Rules and rituals can appear to be a hurdle for newcomers. The coach should be aware of that and supply some simple help. Doing so, it doesn't help to tell the whole difficult framework of rules at once and expect the beginner to memorize it. Successful learning needs experience; it will come step by step.

There are exceptions: Rules of everyday life that can be assumed. For example: Join the circle in the middle of the gym when all the others are already sitting there, without the need of an extra invitation – or stay quiet when somebody else is talking.

In general, children learn best from a positive example. The trainer is needed to live the rituals and rules himself. This very often is a

problem, but while it may be okay to forget a bow to the partner in an adult's training group, it's a serious mistake with a kid's group.

Rules

As already mentioned rules offer support, safety and a stable framework. They are the basis for freedom, creativity, easy-going times and fun. Clearly defined boundaries give the chance to move freely within the limits. They even give the opportunity to sometimes forget about them for a little while, since everyone knows how to behave afterwards.

As few rules as possible, as many as needed

If the set of rules is too big to be easily memorized, if commitments are not understandable or are not consistently handled, they will be counterproductive for good training. In best cases, rules are worded in positive terms instead of the sentence: "Do not do..."

Forbidden things become more interesting, and the sentence: "don't climb up the rope" might wake an idea that hasn't even been in the heads of the kids before. Whatever gets attention grows in importance, so take care not to stick with too many negative statements.

The canon of rules therefore has to be transparent and precise, and it has to be followed very consistently.

Consequence

It's highly important to enforce rituals. They are not negotiable, but part of the group work and have to be accepted. The coach can explain them; discuss their impact, but never the rule itself. There is no questioning – who wants to attend the training has to accept this basis.

The set of rules and rituals can be modernized and adapted to the situation, but this is definitely not a task done by the group, and absolutely not by the parents watching the lesson from the bench, and it absolutely never happens during the training time.

List of rituals

The standards we use in our training are really very small:

- We greet traditionally at the beginning and end of the training. This is taken very seriously and we literally celebrate it.
- Every exercise with a partner begins with a respectful greeting.
- Clear start- and stop-signals: That would be "Hajime" and "Yame" in our Karate-groups and comparable commands in other martial arts styles.

As an anchor we install the centre of the gym: Whenever there is a break, the whole group meets there, sitting in a circle, not talking. This helps a lot to gather attention and raise concentration.

Traditional clothes and suits

Any martial arts style brings its own tradition, and the vast majority also has its own uniform. Like school uniforms, especially in children's groups, the need for traditional clothing (often quite expensive to purchase) is very likely to become a matter of discussion. In our experience it does make sense to decide on a dress code for the dojo members. It supports the idea of community, it visualizes the equality of all the participants in training (although coloured belts may reduce that effect) – and it brings an Asian atmosphere to the room.

A decisive factor is cleanliness and the avoidance of potential injuries. Cleanly cut toe and fingernails, freshly washed clothes, no rolled-up pants or sleeves – and if it is needed (children grow fast, the parents may decide to buy clothes with some reserve) they should be rolled on the inside, and never, never, never fixed with needles (no kidding – we did have that problem!).

Children usually demand a uniform after attending some lessons. They do want to belong to the group and getting the suit becomes some kind of reward and positive confirmation.

A coach should mention when a kid wears his or her suit for the first time in training. These seemingly small things are very important to the children.

Dojokun

Most martial arts have rules written out in full that describe the behaviour in the dojo and with each other. Shotokan Karate usually relies on a "Dojokun" that has been legitimized by the founder of the style, Gichin Funakoshi. In Germany many dojos have it not only on the wall in the gym, but they also recite it before the start of their training.

It surely does no harm to the kids if they learn early what rules have to be respected in the dojo. But especially with the youngest children it doesn't usually help to stubbornly use the traditional rules – they are often hard to understand, even for adults, and need interpretation.

Usually it works pretty well to develop an own Dojokun together with the complete team of trainers. These rules should not only apply to the children, but also for adolescents and adults in training.

It's important for trainers to take these rules really seriously and they should not shy away from extending their usage to any visitor in the dojo. This includes parents as well as watchers. We already mentioned how difficult it can be to deal with those groups – especially for inexperienced coaches.

A written Dojokon helps with this a lot. It takes away the need to explain misbehavior, since it's very easy to refer to the rules that are made for everyone visiting, regardless if attending the training or just watching.

This is an example of a Dojokun for children and parents, used in the Venture Dragon Karate Dojos, led by Patrick:

Dojo-Kun for the children:

1. Always be polite.
2. Bow whenever you enter or leave the dojo.
3. Do not leave the dojo during training without the permission of the instructor.
4. Bow before and after exercise towards your partners.
5. No eating or drinking in the dojo.
6. No jewellery or similar items during training.
7. Keep your Gi and yourself clean.
8. Keep your fingernails and toenails short.
9. Refrain from violent and uncontrolled behavior.
10. To promote the true spirit of martial arts, strive for:
    - Mental development and a good character.
    - Physical development and good health.
    - Improvement of your skills in Karate.
    - Respect and courtesy to others
    - Modesty.
11. If you criticize, do it face to face with only four eyes.

初心

Dojo-Kun for parents:

1. We treat each other politely.
2. We respect the privacy of male and female changing rooms. Daddies use the boy's changing room to pass through to the dojo – Mummies use the girl's changing room.
3. I know that I can watch the first lessons, but afterwards I try to leave my children alone so they can concentrate on the training.
4. Being a watcher I am quiet, don't talk on the phone and never eat or drink.
5. No street shoes in the gym.
6. Criticisms are always resolved in private with the coach or the dojo chief – after the lesson.
7. The trainers will take time for questions before and after training, but never in between.
8. I bring my child to the training at the scheduled beginning of the lesson and pick up afterwards – not one hour before or later.

6. Techniques and exams

Learning and practicing techniques, forms, combinations and/or drills is part of most martial arts styles. It's especially pronounced in the traditional Japanese styles of Karate and Judo, in which the training of techniques for many reasons became a central theme. But also in Ju Jitsu, learning a repertoire plays an important role, and even Ninjutsu or Kung Fu forms (like WingTsun) own a canon of forms and movements that have to be learned and ingrained.

In most cases, the decision for this standard is the programme for belt exams dictated by the association the school or dojo belongs to which are usually suited much more to adults than to children. It's also adjusted for the completion rules of the association.

Teachers of some martial arts can consider themselves to be fortunate, since their style already caters to children. Judo for example is a great style for kids.

In most Karate styles the high priority of children's training is mostly just postulated, not really implemented. The German "Deutscher Karate-Verband" for example published a specialised collection of Shotokan style exams for kids which were really just simplified and reduced versions of the adults´ programme. They also offer what they call a 'style of its own', basically a concept from Italy aimed to fit children's needs much better. It is called "Sound Karate", and it's actually just some aerobic training that has nothing to do with Karate anymore: Punching colourful balls, completing a circuit training of gymnastic exercises and things like that.

Bonsai exams vs. colour exams

We've already stated that the training of techniques should not be the centre of martial arts exercises for kids. The younger the children, the more holistic lessons should be in our opinion. Specialization, performance orientation and technical training should increase with the age of the participants.

Therefore we recommend developing your own examination concept for the Bonsai groups, taking into account the actual training content.

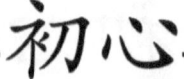

We have had good experiences in keeping the 5- to 8-year-olds away from classical belt testing as specified by the official Karate federation. In our Karate groups the children all wear white belts, but there are exams in regular intervals for which they receive a certificate.

These exams are important as a confirmation of good performance, as extrinsic motivation and above all to give parents and grandparents the chance to pull out the camera and document the achievements of the youngest family members.

For the children themselves every exam is a good chance to get used to pressure, to cope with nervousness and stage fright in front of a big audience.

This also prepares them for the official exams, following the rules of the Karate federation, which we usually start at the age of eight. This changes training in general since these exams demand higher technical skills and practicing them reduces the scope for incorporating other topics. There is simply less time for playing and talking if the group has time pressure to get things done for a technical exam.

At this time it pays off if the coaches have succeeded in making even boring or uniformed parts of the training an interesting experience for the kids; wrapping them up in playful tasks or giving the them the chance to explore the background of techniques rather than just

drilling in a standardized movement. A well-told story explaining the reason for a certain movement is much better than a reasonable description of what to do with each body part involved, as adults usually want to hear it.

It is recommended to make this change very clear. For example, the "Bonsai class" is for the youngest kids, "children's class" for the older ones and a dedicated "adolescent's classes" as a next step. Usually the last group of participants is also very happy about not being "kids" anymore, but still not having to be "adult" and training with all those boring grown-ups.

In any case we suggest separating "Bonsai exams" from "Colour exams", as most martial arts usually combine a change of colour with any exam.

Transition

The transition from Bonsai exams to Colour exams (or from Bonsai class to Children's class) may be devised in different ways. It heavily depends on the structure of the groups, the number of classes available in the dojo, the room and coach availability to open additional classes.

Option 1: Exam of a complete Bonsai class

If your Bonsai classes are sorted by age, it may be a good decision to allow a whole group of children to have their first colour exam and then switch to the Children's classes. This maintains the structure of the peer group with its very own momentum. The downside: If someone is missing at the date of the exam or fails to meet all the requirements, this may become a burden for the whole class. It's a test of authority to leave a single kid behind in a Bonsai class, while the rest of the group is promoted to the next level, and it may be even worse to transfer a kid that is not ready yet, since this can lead to real frustration and set a bad example for the other participants.

Option 2: Individual participants make the change

In this case the coaching staff designates individual participants to do the next step as soon as they met the requirements. This increases the difficulties during training for the coaches, since it's never the whole group prepared for the next exam, but it does leave open the option to introduce new participants in the Bonsai class at any time.

For the trainers, with this option comes the unpleasant task of telling every single kid whether he or she is ready or not to fulfil the requirements of a colour exam and the Children's class, or if it is better to stay in the Bonsai class for a while longer.

Unfortunately the major disadvantage of this approach is the constant fluctuation inside both groups, which tears apart peer groups and cliques of friends. Usually the switch from one class to another also means a change of training times, and this influences the schedule of kids as well as parents and may lead to children leaving.

Option 3: Bonsai exams as preparation for Colour exams

In this case the dojo defines a number of Bonsai exams as a basic requirement to attend a colour exam. Whoever successfully accomplishes, for example four Bonsai exams, can start preparation for their first colour exam – and switch to the children's group as soon as he passes this exam.

Contents of the Bonsai exams

A dojo that decides to incorporate separate Bonsai exams needs to prepare them solidly and thoughtfully. If the training for the youngest kids is holistic and covers various topics such as sports, self assertion, social skills and background knowledge, this should also apply for the exams.

It's important in any kind of exam (especially with the youngest martial artists) to understand that failing an exam means the trainee was poorly prepared. And that is, in most cases, the responsibility of the trainer rather than the participant. Whoever fails an exam should not have started it. Children who are unable to cope with the requirements should not appear for exams. If they slipped through, for whatever reason, or simply are overwhelmed by nervousness, it is the job if the examiner to guide them carefully through the examination process – without mercy, but in a way that they can succeed in the end.

Exams given away without effort or achievement are worth nothing and should definitely be avoided.

Repertoire of techniques

What techniques can be tested? Generally all things that have been practiced in everyday lessons. The criteria to decide whether the

performance of a trainee is "good" or at least "good enough" should be handled very differently from regular colour exams.

In general, children get bored in pure techniques training. They only partially understand the importance of performing a movement with high precision.

"We already did that" can be heard if techniques are repeated the second or third time. "I already mastered that" is a favourite sentence of boys who dislike being confronted with their own shortcomings.

One big challenge is the distinction between "left" and "right". The younger the children, the more difficult it is. The differentiation of aiming zones on an opponent's body can also be challenging for young children to grasp and real tactical practice can very quickly turn into a brawl.

A fast change of pace is helpful, fast enough to prevent the kids from being bored. On the other hand even the youngest children definitely have to learn how to focus, and of course they need to develop frustration tolerance when it comes to repetition in training and the assessment of their performance.

The 'correct' execution of given tasks may really be limited by age and the learning ability of the participants. That is even truer when considering the appearance, every now and then, of extraordinarily talented youngsters in classes. They are not proving the opposite, but just are the opposite: an exception.

These talented kids are often the result of high ambitions, sometimes driven by the parents rather than the child his or herself. Generating high achievements by pressure is not the goal of Bonsai martial arts.

Methodology is the most important weapon of a Bonsai trainer, and that requires creativity. The coach needs a variety of ideas on how to teach certain techniques from different approaches:

- Games/forms of play that lead to techniques, stances, basic forms or combinations, should be developed and varied.

- Technical content or the topics of upcoming exams can be melted into other areas of the training in a way that the children don't experience them as the "boring reasonable part" of the training, in competition with the "exciting fun parts".

- Approach with techniques that can include high levels of creativity for the kids: The trainer offers physical challenges or fighting tasks, and the children can develop their own solutions, carefully guided by the trainer to find the "right" technique, combination, stance or strategy. This leads to successful experiences by finding a solution for a problem and ensures that the participants understand what they are doing rather than just "dancing" given movements in a boring, repetitive way.

- Never and under no circumstances should the lesson be divided into "working" and "fun". Some coaches end up in this trap, saying things like: "If you work hard now, we can play a game afterwards". This kills motivation rather than supporting it – and it guarantees the most important parts of martial arts training are experienced as hard work without fun by the kids.

Against common expectations many participants of our Bonsai classes state that they especially like the technique training, since they learn something new and really have the feeling of getting better. Therefore it seems that even constant repetition and hard work can be handled in a way that it is still fun and not just an annoying burden.

In our train-the-trainer workshops "Bonsai-Kampfkunstlehrer" we usually develop methods and very practical approaches with the participating teachers, always connected to their own style of martial arts. It is difficult to meet the full range of martial arts in a book like this, but nevertheless you will find some example lessons in the appendix of this book.

(Mental) fatigue

We've probably already mentioned it very clearly: In martial arts technique is important. It serves the learning of movement patterns, increases coordination and supports endurance training - physical as well as mental, since the repetition of movements is exhausting also on a mental level.

There is one remark that is often told to coaches working with adult students: "Stamina equals concentration". Considering this fact, the repetition and practice of technical skills should not be used to raise endurance – although every martial artist knows exemptions from this rule that didn't only work, but also were a great deal of fun.

Training with children needs modification of this rule, since sports medicine has collected evidence that kids get tired to a much lesser extent than adults.

It's easier for them than grown-ups to go beyond their limits and not recognize when they've exhausted their resources.

There are two reasons why this is important to know for any coach:

- It easily happens that children are overstrained. They are not aware of their physical limits, and they don't feel tired in the way adults do. This fact bears health risks any trainer has to pay attention to.

- The growing numbers of children we see in everyday lessons who are nevertheless permanently tired or sluggish, are not *physically* exhausted. They show learned behaviour, a mental fatigue. It is a lack of concentration and a lack of will to work hard for something you want to achieve.

We already mentioned before how much virtualization and de-bodification of our lives lead exactly to these symptoms of laziness, physically as well as mentally. During training it is therefore highly important to find a balance between presenting something new and exciting every time – and yet prevent the lesson from switching to just a non-challenging fun-event.

It has to be learned to practice persevering and to cope with tasks that seem to be boring. In the best case children find out about the great value of physical activity and how satisfying it can be to master a technique. The trainer has to help the kids discover how unimportant it is to make their movements LOOK good, to leave a great impression doing it, and how important it is what they feel and experience themselves doing a movement.

Self-explaining techniques

Intrinsic motivation becomes difficult as soon as form becomes an end in itself as it can happen in many martial arts styles.

While in gymnastics for example it is totally obvious that a more difficult technique needs more work and has a higher value on that scale and while in dancing it is totally understandable that certain movements simply look better or convey a special message to an audience. In martial arts it is really completely unintelligible why a motion should be practiced in this and only this artificial, traditional way, while during a fight you have to move absolutely in a different anyway.

There may be many reasons for this contradiction: Practicing forms and techniques are meant as basic education, they teach athletic skills, they help develop a proper use of force and physical power, they are a good school for the mind and a challenge for the endurance of the practitioner. Many forms reveal themselves only by years of active practice.

Great reasons and arguments that leave kids completely unimpressed. They enjoy training techniques as long as

- they work pretty well (usually not the case during training),
- they look great (very often rather detrimental if you want to do it right rather than just cool) or
- if they understand what they can do with the movement they are working on.

Techniques that are learned through a practical task, that make sense, have a meaning and a good effect, are most interesting.

The alternative: Wrap the learning of new movement in an interesting package. Use games that lead step by step to the desired movement, or tell a nice story that explains the single part of the movement.

Waiting periods

Perhaps the most important task for a trainer team is not the teaching of the martial arts style itself – but to create a motivating learning environment. This includes the right surrounding conditions. Martial arts training offers personal discoveries far beyond athletic education.

One huge challenge for the kids is waiting. Whenever there are times during the lesson when they can not be active but have to be patiently watching somebody else this can become an ordeal, especially for lively children.

A good way to prevent waiting periods is the introduction of a circuit training, whenever there is a need of teaching things that can't be done altogether at the same time. This gives the chance to keep the participants occupied all at once and punching mitts or punching bags can be introduced which are usually not available for every single child in a group.

If you go for a set of parallel exercises like this, it is important to take care that they have an equivalent value. Otherwise the more interesting events draw the attention away from the apparently less attractive.

In cases where there is no chance for solutions like a circuit, the following rules apply:

For the trainer: Several short queues rather than one long row.

For the kids: Don't disturb other children while queuing.

It's completely unimportant that the waiting children are standing sorted in ranks or are absolutely quiet. As long as they don't disturb

others and pay attention when it comes to their own turn, they can talk or play.

Methodological examples

We have already explained how important it is to prevent a contradiction between the practice of techniques and the playful part of a lesson. Too quickly this would raise the impression that technique is the dry, boring part of martial arts; a bitter pill that has to be swallowed. A good trainer embeds the hard working parts of a lesson in a way that games and learning, playing and repetitive practice melt into each other and the difference is barely noticed by the kids.

In the following we give some examples – they are just ideas, nothing else, since every martial arts style needs its own approach. The experience of our seminars regarding Bonsai training shows how different approaches can be very successful – and they also demonstrate how there are no boundaries for creativity.

<u>Coordinative approach</u>

Coordinative tasks – important in martial arts in general – can be well placed inside playful approaches:

- Kicks:
    - Running games in which the aim is to stand on one leg.
    - More difficult exercises that include standing on one leg and taking challenging positions with the other one. Examples: Lifting the leg in front of the body to the chest, lifting it to the side, lifting it to the side with the lower leg parallel to the ground, "like a dachshund wanting to pee" (this description usually leads to a lot of laughter and some concerned looks by parents watching from the bench – Karate-teachers know that this position is a good start for learning the traditional Mawashi-Geri of the Shotokan style.)
    - The next step is a certain movement with the leg lifted in the air.
    - In games like this it can be the challenge that everyone who makes a mistake has to drop out from the game.
    - Once the children notice how difficult the movement can be, the coach can help with hints to make it easier or

better looking. This usually is a lot of fun, especially when a tricky task is mastered successfully on this approach.
- At the very end the coach can disclose the fact that the exercise was indeed a new kick, having a name and a certain way to do it right.
- It makes sense to give the kids a chance to try the kick instantly in a more realistic way, on a punching bag, for example, or on a gymnastic mat that is leaned against the wall. This gives the opportunity to experience the effectiveness and understand the connection between technique and application.

- The art of falling:
  - A great way of introducing fall exercises are competitive games that demand the children to cross a mat area in defined positions: One hand has to be on the ground all the time or only one foot is allowed on the ground at a time, or no foot at all is allowed to touch the mat (in this case the kids have to roll).
  - An alternative would be to cross the mat area rolling forwards or backwards.
  - In this approach the trainer doesn't show how to do a fall exercise the right way, but instead gives useful hints how to make the competition more successful, faster, more efficient, less exhausting. This connects the technique to its application and delivers additional motivation for practising.
  - Of course here you can also use all those well-known little exercises that are so popular in ground-oriented grappling-styles: Rolling over a bench, using a partner as a barrier or things like that.
  - This playful approach reduces the complexity of falling techniques – at least from the kids´ point of view. It focuses on a result that the children really want to achieve, which helps to prevent learning blocks. The disadvantage of this idea is the alternative movement patterns that the participants may propose as an alternative to what they should learn from the teacher's point of view. This needs some sensitivity and the ability to accept new ideas – as well as the ability to lead back to the desired movements when it comes to repetition.

- Alternative:
    - Starting a brainstorming session: How to fall dramatically without hurting yourself. Two kids work together, one of them performing a takedown, the other falling in slow motion. Making a big show is allowed, the aim is to fall in a way that doesn't hurt. The trainer's job is to add ideas to reduce risks. After a while he can raise the speed of throwing as well as falling.
    - The last step is a competition: Which one of the couples working together is able to fall the most often in a given period of time. It's very obvious to the children that the goal is to fall as gentle as possible at maximum speed, so both partners will stay healthy and fit. The trainer can support this idea by mentioning matters of respect and responsibility for their own health.
- Stances and Walking:
    - In many martial arts great emphasis is placed on basic positions and stances, very often also on certain ways of moving forward. Many trainers, examiners and last but not least competition referees, care a great deal about static positions – usually the final form of a movement. How much sense that makes for the training in general (also for adults), is a separate question (we have serious doubts), but there are a great deal of games to practice movements as well as positions.
    - The easiest start: Duel. Any kind of position or stance should bring serious benefits, since that is why they were introduced into martial arts in the beginning. The job of the trainer is to develop struggle exercises that give the participants a chance to feel these benefits. Referring to Shotokan Karate as an example: Zenkutsu-Dachi is very usable to push somebody – Kokutsu-Dachi, on the other hand, is a good way to pull someone since he puts weight and power on the rearmost leg. A fighting game could demand exactly this from the kids: To pull or to push an opponent or perhaps pull or push large objects. This also makes the upright, straight position of the torso plausible, since any bending leads to imbalance.
    - Playing tag can be used to introduce traditional stances and positions: Whoever is caught has to put himself into one of the given positions and has to stay that way until

somebody else sets him free. One good approach for the famous Kiba-Dachi of Karate (a horse-riding stance) is the game "Trolls and fairies": The fairies are running free in the room, while the trolls try to catch them. Whenever they succeed, the caught fairy is magically turned into a tree, rooted strongly into the soil, which of course means: Taking the Kiba-Dachi position. Another fairy can set the tree free by sliding or crawling beneath its legs – a good reason to really spread the legs wide and take a deep position close to the ground. The trainer can give helpful hints to make the stance more efficient or how to endure it over a longer period of time.

- "One – two – three – Sayonara": One child is standing back to the group, facing a wall. She or he uses this sentence and turns around right after the word "Sayonara". In this very moment all the other kids have to take a correct basic position and are not allowed to shake or move at all. Whoever is caught moving or making a mistake in any stance has to start from the beginning.

- Body tension and coordination:
  - Exercises borrowed from BrainGym or similar coordinative training models are very useful for martial arts training. They can be part of the warm-up.
  - Techniques carried out on very soft gymnast mats, on the small side of a bench or on rolled-out belts/ropes increase body-awareness and coordinative abilities.
  - Carrying exercises that demand the children to keep their body completely stiff while being transported are a great way to exercise body tension. One highlight in our classes is the assembly line game: Every child in the group is carried above all the other participants of the class (see games collection in chapter 7).

- Movement tasks:
  - These tasks can be introduced using small stories: The kids are asked to move like a cat (quiet, softly, lightly) to exercise a new stance. Candles can be blown out with a punch without touching the flame to practice fast arm-techniques. A balloon can be kept in the air using kicks.

- To teach more complex movement patterns, it may be helpful to use Clap-hand-games, in which the kids have to touch each others hands in a certain sequence.

Application as entry to techniques

Self-explaining techniques are the most easy to explain – and vice versa every technique has a certain use or application. To teach new movements from this point of view ("what can I do with it?") is helpful in any training, including adolescents or adults. The traditional Asian way of "do first what you are told to do, and later ask why you should do it" is not really applicable for most Western learners, and especially not for children who like to ask questions and are encouraged to do so in school or kindergarten.

- Takedowns and Joint Locks:
  - Fighting games are the easiest way to introduce takedowns as well as joint locks. You may find a lot of different ideas in our games list in chapter 7. It is easy to find connection points from brawling to well-prepared techniques that can be trained and used to get a hold of an opponent, to control him or – on the opposite – to free yourself from somebody trying to do exactly that. Same applies to the way to bring somebody else down to the ground, preferably without hurting him.
  - A very good idea is to include the children into the process of discovering the right way to do it. They usually have many ideas and proposals that can easily be "refined" by the trainer.
  - Advanced participants get a chance of explaining their own knowledge to others. This kind of peer tutoring also has positive effects on the ones teaching.
- Punches and strikes:
  - Hitting balloons or balls in the air, aiming to handle the impact in exactly the right moment, alternatively to stop the ball right on the spot or hit it so hard that it flies a maximum range.
  - It is so simple that it is often surprising why so few dojos really practice that way: Using a punching bag or a punching mitt, perhaps even a gymnastic mat leaned

against a wall in the gym. Punches (as well as kicks) are best when they are really efficient, and a technique practiced with real tactile feedback is better than one just hit to the air. Besides all that: It's simply fun and it helps to get rid of aggression and pressure. The trainer will enjoy the fact that he just has to give some hints to increase efficiency or reduce pain caused by the impact.

- Blocks:
    o Plain truth: Blocks are best trained when used to defend from an actual attack. By giving an attack and asking the kids for a solution to this challenge, the trainer can introduce an interesting problem, trigger the creativity of the participants and help find a real working solution. Main rules: Efficiency and the best way to prevent the body from being hurt. From this direction it is possible to approach the classical movement pattern of their own martial arts style.
    o It makes sense to explore possibilities of using a block not only as a defence, but at the same time as a counter technique.
    o It is even better to connect a whole system of movement to the block itself, for example a consistent evasion to the right direction, a step inside the opponents body, or even taking up the technique of the attacker and using it, perhaps for a takedown. All these things can be trained step by step in a way that gives the children a chance to unfold their creativity.
    o An excellent result would be the ability to use a block at the same time as a liberation from grips or attempted joint locks. It doesn't matter if this happens in a very free form – even things that adults would call "a bit far out" are still a fascinating adventure for children.

Deepening and repetition

It's a reasonable end for any lesson to draw a conclusion: The coach shows the kids how much they achieved in the lesson they just finished. This can be combined with a short repetition, stripped down to the technique, without any story or methodological tricks.

The next lesson can start in the same manner: A short repetition of the last training is a good start and it helps those participants who missed the last time to catch up, even if this might be more exhausting to them, since they missed the great pedagogical introduction.

This also offers a chance: Children who already know the techniques can explain (and show) them to those who don't. This usually leads to even more learning for the ones explaining than for the ones listening.

Some ideas for repetition:

- Tippkick: Two children practice together, one naming techniques, the other one doing the movement. The command is not given verbally, but by tipping the shoulder. This signal can be coded: One tip means a punch, two tips mean a kick, three tips mean a punch with the opposite hand and so on. This gives a good chance to combine multiple techniques in one exercise and at the same time guarantees a high focus and good concentration.

- Slow motion: Movements should be executed as slow as possible, and of course as perfect as possible. This also works fine with forms (like Katas in Karate).

- Modelling: A group of kids have the task to shape one partner into exactly the right position. The model does not move at all, he just follows the instructions given without any words. This helps the kids to understand the reason for certain positions and movements.

- Last but not least: Punching bag or punching mitts are a great way for repetition and the deepening of movements.

初心

7. Background knowledge

Martial arts are based on ancient roots, and they are in most cases strongly anchored in Asian culture, and as we already mentioned before: This guarantees a proper "cool factor" in the eyes of the children.

Our ShoShin Bonsai concept uses this certain factor already in its name: "Bonsai" are fully developed trees, but extremely small. They are cared for with great devotion and every single one of them is a piece of art on its own.

A shortcoming of this name is the fact that Bonsai trees are never allowed to grow. They are kept tiny using a lot of effort, which is of course the opposite of what we want to do to our children. In addition, Bonsais are full grown trees, just featuring a small shape, and that is what children are not: They are not small adults and they need to be treated very differently from grown-ups during lessons.

All this shows how tricky it can be to transport Asian ideas straight to a Western environment. It can lead to a lot of misunderstandings, since Judeo-Christian thinking is shaped by many premises that are not a part of Asian traditional culture.

Buddhism for example doesn't see charity as the core of its philosophy, which is a huge difference to Christian ideas. Instead the main goal is the elimination of the ego to gain freedom. Of course this is a very shortened description and only part of the truth, but it may be helpful to recognize the huge differences in philosophy and general ideas. Karate for example embeds many features of Zen Buddhism that some westerners find hard to deal with sometimes.

Properly prepared, martial arts can be an interesting door to this kind of knowledge. There is more to explore than just athletic technique, and there are valuable aspects of Asian philosophy that can be used in everyday life, too – if wanted.

But what does that mean for the concrete, practical Karate lessons? And how far is this important for training with children?

Which kind of knowledge?

It's a surprising thing how in many martial arts lessons the teaching of background knowledge leads to endless lectures about completely dead facts from an ancient past. Facts that have no practical value for training, nor in everyday life outside the dojo. They are not interesting, not even for adult students – and kids should be saved completely from this kind of experience.

For example: A list of all Karate masters, reaching from Okinawa to Japan in the last century and perhaps even China before that, is completely unimportant. Yes, some trainers like to use that kind of information to show off, but they do not help the students. Maybe it is of some use for high-ranked teachers who are exploring the roots of their own style, like the discovery that Bassai Dai in Shotokan looks so different from its ancestor Passai because of the very bulky appearance of Master Itosu, who developed the kata that is practiced today in Shotokan style. This little detail could be used as proof for the importance of finding ones own, individual approach to martial arts that suits personal needs.

This is exactly the kind of information that is of only limited use for kid's training. The same applies to extensive use of Chinese, Japanese or Korean terms or names that are hard to memorize and in most cases don't help the learning. An advanced martial artist may profit from knowing Japanese names of techniques, since they sometimes convey more information than the translated term.

Knowledge for knowledge sake, therefore, serves no purpose. Instead, every piece of information given should be helpful for further learning. Each content of the lesson should have a close connection to the actual martial art, to rituals, to behavioral rules or at least to real life outside the dojo. As an alternative, knowledge can be something exciting, interesting that generates an atmosphere and an authentic mood – children are usually proud if they are able to count to ten in Japanese or know some Chinese characters.

In general, what should be well known by every martial artist are not so much facts of language and historical background, but above all the rules, rituals and ways of thinking, as we have already explained in the chapter "Violence Prevention". The first step towards philosophy in martial arts is the questioning of one's own behavior. And it starts with the question of violence and aggression, because it is inherent to the system contained in martial arts.

The teacher as role model

The trainer may talk a lot – but whatever he or she tells, it will only reach a ratio of the students. But what really works are emotional messages, they are received more easily and stick in the mind much better. Of all ways to learn on an emotional level, practical experience is the most efficient. Whatever is not only seen or heard, but actually physically felt, is remembered most intensely. At this rate a really good teacher talks less – and shows more. Martial artists especially should never underestimate their own influence as a role model.

If there is a lack for practical examples about any topic, a well-told story is better than boring reasonable information. Only bore the kids if it is absolutely inevitable.

Example information

Simple truth: Deliver information first that is asked by the kids. Attention is caught best with issues that are really interesting for the children. There are plenty of topics that come up again and again during our Bonsai lessons. Here are some popular examples:

Why do we wear these uniforms?

Whatever the looks of your traditional training uniform – as long as you don't wear informal sports clothes during lessons – this question will pop up after a while. It is more difficult to answer in very traditional styles, since often enough the uniform just reflects ancient traditions which are not valued as much in the eyes of young children. (The same applies to adolescents – constant complaints about fashionable inadequacies of a do-gi are very often reasons for serious criticism, especially from girls.)

In fact, any kind of uniform documents the belonging to a certain group and the will to accept its rules. The suit also equalizes all the members of a dojo, since nobody can shine by using jewelry or special accessories. While in the gym, we are all travellers with the same goal and we can distinguish by performance and behaviour. There is not even a difference between men and women while wearing a gi.

Will we learn to fight with weapons too?

Weapons are intriguing to children – even to those who are already adult by age. Nevertheless they are not part of all the martial arts-systems, which doesn't mean they can't be used from time to time as an incentive anyway.

In styles that usually do not use weapons, they run the risk that playing with these tools starts to compete with the real contents of everyday training. Too many trainers of Karate for example seem to use weapon training to cover the lack of depth in their own Karate knowledge and prevent their students from getting bored by endless repetitions. This is surely the wrong way.

Swords, sticks, ninja throwing stars, Tonfas are highly inviting to try out to see what is possible by using them – and they are also feeding the "cool factor" we referred to previously. Used in the right way weapons training can also support the actual lessons. Shinai lessons for example (bambus-swords, used mostly in sword-fighting martial arts) are a great way to practice endurance, develop fighting skills and concentration.

What's my sign?

The Chinese use a different zodiac system from the European one, and that is a great example of cultural diversity. Since animals take a huge place in Asian philosophy as well as in martial arts, the connection is a good approach for interesting discussions with the kids.

It's easy to find a simple book from a supermarket about Chinese zodiac signs. Research on this topic can form part of a "homework" for children so it gives a simple a way of introducing a whole new idea. And animals also offer a great approach for practical training, since the comparison of techniques or strategies with the habits of certain animals is very comprehensible in the eyes of children.

Martial arts in general refer to very different sorts of animals. Learning a classical animal-style (like many Kung Fu styles) makes it easy to build the connection. Shotokan Karate is called "tiger" style, and even if that is for different reasons, this visualization can be used very well during lessons. "Karate is not an elephant-style", is one of the typical sentences. "We don't need to stamp the ground, we try to walk quiet like a cat. A huge, dangerous cat."

It is also interesting to explore forms, katas or combinations for hints to which animal could be hidden inside of them. Not always are the results of these explorations really authentic and connected to the ancient ideas, but it helps to trigger creativity, ideas and open the mind of the children for a deeper understanding of what they are doing.

In our Shotokan lessons we refer to five "fighting animals", as they are taught by Gojy-Ryu grand master Fritz Nöpel: Tiger, Leopard, Snake, Dragon and Crane. This group can be widened as much as needed (if your style allows you to do so), but these five animals already offer a lot of different ideas for an interesting training.

Why do we have that ritual greeting in the beginning and the end of a lesson?

The greeting ritual seems to be of special interest to children as well as parents. It attracts a lot of questions and needs to be carefully explained – especially in Germany, where everything that seems to be military is always a matter of concern.

The greeting is a reminder of the roots of martial arts and the tradition to which we belong. It also reminds us of the responsibility we have: The responsibility of the teacher who has to work hard since he carries all the knowledge of his own teachers and their masters – and the responsibility of the students who have to focus on the training and the art they are learning. The group in general carries responsibility too: Every single member has a duty towards all others and for the own behavior, so everybody can feel well and safe being a part of the dojo community. Of course that is a special demand towards the older students, who also are a role model for the ones who started later.

The exact form of the greeting is very different, depending on martial art and style – and it tends to vary depending on the teacher, too. Some only sit for a few seconds, closing their eyes for a short period of times (like in Judo), others perform a long ritual to wake up the dojo spirits, clapping their hands and reciting certain sentences (as in many Ninjutsu-styles).

No matter what way you choose: It is a helpful moment especially for children. It supports the arrival in the gym and the switching to the right state of mind for a concentrated lesson, and it delivers the quietness that many kids are missing so much in modern, noisy times.

Beginning with this very moment, the world stays outside the doors of the gym. During training nothing else counts, the world may come back with the greeting at the end of the lesson. Therefore creating mental relaxation and a guarantee for full-focused training.

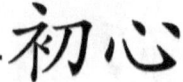

Who's that grandpa in the picture?

This refers to Gichin Funakoshi, the founder of the Shotokan Karate style. In our dojos we have a picture of him on the wall, sometimes he is even part of a little shrine.

As much as the question sounds disrespectful, in most cases it is really just curiosity. The cutest example we witnessed was when the picture was missing one day and a little boy asked: "What happened to Kawasaki today?"

What we explain to our Bonsai kids: Gichin Funakoshi is the great-grandfather of our Karate, the man who made sure that we are all able to learn Shotokan today. He joins us in our training, so he has a chance to watch our work and see that we are really carrying on with his Karate. A running gag in our dojos is the fact that from time to time he looses his footing and hangs crooked in the frame since he is unhappy with what he had to witness. While in reality this happens due to the weak glue we used inside the frame, it is always a big deal for the children when it happens.

How many belts are there? In which order?

Even if coloured belts are not worn in the Bonsai groups of our dojo, this question is highly intriguing for children – partly because the team of trainers of course has differently colored belts. The most fascinating fact in our Karate dojo remains that there are many black belts, but they do not change their color anymore... by being used so much the colour vanishes after a while.

Where on the globe is Asia? Where is China? And where is Japan?

Of course this questions may vary if you are actually practicing Korean, Thai or Filipino martial arts, but in general it stays exciting: How far away is Asia from us, and how are they related to each other? The difference in size between China and Japan is always a reason for astonishment – and since our dojos are situated in Germany, it's always a great discovery that Europe is quite small on the globe, and Germany is even smaller.

Where do martial arts come from?

We usually explain it by showing a map to demonstrate how martial arts moved from India via China to Okinawa and Japan and to other places – but we also mention the similar developments in Europe and America and how the cultural differences influenced the development of fighting skills in the Western and the Eastern world.

What is a samurai?

The history of Japanese knights and their role in the feudalist Japanese society is always a good way to discuss Japanese culture and the basis of many traditions still alive in the martial arts – at least in those from Japan. Children are usually most interested in clothing, weapons and food of the Samurai, and it's a great idea to compare them to the lifestyle of European knights. We strongly recommend using pictures or even a video.

Storytelling

The best way to transfer knowledge to children is a good story. The book "Karate-Do" by Gichin Funakoshi for example is an interesting source for stories – although it is not good for reading, since it is written too complicated.

The stories themselves are nevertheless exactly the kind of tales children love – simple, straightforward and always with some moral advice that can be discussed.

Singing songs, painting pictures or similar artistic activities also work fine. Admittedly most of the trainers in our dojos simply dislike them and are not up for the task.

Special events

A movie with a group discussion afterwards, painting tattoos with Chinese characters or a Halloween party are good working ideas to invite the children (and perhaps their parents, siblings and friends) for a chance to know more about martial arts background.

More specific for martial arts are certain events covering a certain form/kata, with its history, background, applications and perhaps a search for the five elements or animal forms connected to the form – whatever your specific martial art offers as an interesting approach.

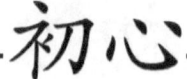

This kind of workshop can also be the basis for a weekend away from home.

Following our own experiences, this kind of event is also a good opportunity to involve families: Father/son-weekends for example are always booked solid weeks before the actual event starts.

8. Games

Games in the martial arts training are, for purists, a reason for discussion. We also knew times when warming-up games were forbidden. At one time our motto was 'Wildly swinging arms and cheerful ball competitions are incompatible with martial arts'. During our apprenticeships as coaches we had learned the probability for injuries at warming-up games is way too high.

However, this basic attitude remained just a temporary idea.

Interestingly, it first started to crumble in the training for adults. Just like children, adults also have fun and enjoy games and it became noticeable that in a playful way, a tremendous amount of martial art subjects can be worked on.

This does not have to be foolish, and mostly, it does not have to interfere with the "serious" demand of the training. The right choice of game, suited to the 'message' of the lesson, is important and so is taking the time to analyze the results of the game together with the children. In this way, games can be a component for the development of specific subjects. This applies in particular to the Bonsai-training, for which we already defined, as it provides a high ratio of social study, motor skills and physical abilities in general.

Games as a methodical component, not as a reward

A correct approach is required to ensure that variations support the content of the training.

Quite a few coaches for children use the games as a "reward": They inform their pupils, i.e. that there will be a "nice game" at the end of the training, provided that all participate well in the technical training. In that way, the game will become a reward, which can only be achieved by "hard work" – and this consists of the "actual" training.

This argumentation decreases the value of the games (actually being made for pure fun) as well as the technical part of the training (this one is inevitably displeasing).

For each hour, good coaches build up a good mixture of games, exercises, collective efforts and technical training, each component slips into the other, the issues complement each other and are based on one another, there is no split between "actual training" and "fun part". Eventually, the whole hour is oriented to "learning with fun".

The following list of games originates from the practical work of our children's group. This is only a small list of games which can be added to – there is a variety of good compendium of games on the market, including some which are specified for martial arts training.

The burning hall

- Size of the group: 10+
- Materials :
  gymnastic mats,
  adequate space,
  benches, vaulting boxes as obstacles,
  balls (if necessary)

A great game on the issue of teamwork, co-ordination and social cooperation. The children will be divided into groups, which may not be less than five participants in each. Each group will receive two gymnastic mats, which are piled up on top of each other. They must be leveled and touch the wall. The mats of the other groups lay next to them, parallel against the same wall.

Both groups now have the task to reach the other side of the hall. All children have to touch the wall there and after that, return to their starting point. There they will have to touch the wall again.

Does it sound simple? Well, yes it does - but here is the catch:

The coaches will set the hall on fire. Everything is burning, the floor, the walls, the benches and everything else that is located in the hall. The children are only safe under their group-mats.

As soon as a single member of the group touches the fire – it does not matter with what, it could be with their foot or with their hair – the whole group has to return to their starting point, no matter how far the group had already achieved at this point of time. Even, if they would have almost reached the finish.

At this point, teamwork becomes an issue: Children experience different personalities within the group – some will hinder the group because they take too much of a risk, others will be timid and some may even want to lead the group.

In any case, the ones who are normally the most successful and talented participants, who usually score the goals in a football-match, may find it troubling for them as this lesson only works if all of them co-operate with one another.

Taking offence at members who are clumsy, even repeatedly so, does not improve performance. Even worse: As no one in the group is supposed to touch the floor (or anything else in the hall), an offended member of the group who has to remain on the bench makes it a disaster for the entire group. Because they do not get anywhere when team members are missing from the mat.

For simplification, imaginary fire-proofed gloves are provided to the children. Only with these are they permitted to touch the floor, walls and everything else. In that way they are able to lift up the mats, throw them forwards, change the mats, drag the others behind and throw them forward, so that have a way to climb up and repeat the whole thing.

Obstacles can also be pushed aside with their hands, as soon as they recognize that these can be touched. Plenty of obstacles should be present in order not to simplify it too much: benches, vaulting boxes, trampolines and soft mats across the hall require high attention.

If the coaches have the courage, even balls can be put in their way. As these can be touched with the hands, they can be thrown and can make the other teams return to the starting point. However, this quickly will lead to arguments between the groups, as nobody is able to proceed any further.

Important rule : The game is not finished until all groups have definitely arrived. Quitting won't work.

Even better: A quicker success can be achieved, if the teams who are already finished support the other teams, who are still on their way. That is the point where real co-operation is required.

<u>River crossing</u>

- Size of the group: 7+
- Materials:
  pieces of carpet

The game is built up in a similar way as "The hall is burning", but a different issue is important, as the characteristic of competition is at a lower level. On the other hand, in this game the motor abilities are of a higher value - and also the ability to not only care about oneself but also for others.

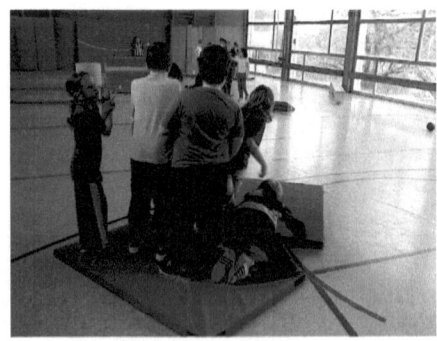

First of all, a river is defined in the hall and it needs to be crossed. The person who steps in the water has to return – but in this case, not the entire group. In order to cross the river, pieces of carpet are issued to the children and these may be thrown into the water. These will remain there, as long as they are touched – with the hands or the legs, it makes no difference.

As soon as they are not touched, they will swim away, in other words: The coaches will pull them off and out of the game. If a high number of pieces of carpet 'swim away' then it will be impossible for the group to successfully continue their river crossing.

All of them will have to arrive, a single individual can not celebrate a victory on his own although he may have made it, as everyone has to think for the entire team and has to keep an eye on several pieces of carpet at once.

Tightly bandaged

- Size of the group: 4+
- Materials:
  ribbons to tighten the legs

In this case it is a foot race, which can be played with any number of children and any number of groups. Each group forms a line, the legs are tightened with ribbons or elastic bands and the objective is to achieve a certain distance together. This will only work well if the children consult each other and take one another with mutual consideration. An obstacle course would definitely make the mission even more difficult.

Pair running

- Size of the group: 2+
- Materials:
  None

This is a warm-up game, which works well in groups of any size. Two children run side by side, one of them is their leader, the other one needs to orientate himself towards the other one.

Various difficulties can be added to the game:

- The one who is following needs to keep track of either the right or the left shoulder of the leader. Wild twists and turns will make it hard for the other. Also, the shoulder can suddenly be changed in between, if such a command is given by the coach.
- The follower has to imitate the leader's movements. The creativity thereby has no limits.

- The follower constantly has to circle around the leader, but this is definitely not easy.

Enchaining the "2"

1. Size of the group: 4+
2. Materials:
   None

The children are lined up in two rows, in the way that each individual has a partner face to face. One row will receive the number '1', the other row the number '2' (optionally different colors, sounds or something else). Now, if the number '1' is announced, the children of this row will try to catch their counterpart. If '2' is announced then vice versa. The ones who need to be tagged are only safe if they can make it to the opposite wall of the gym.

Now, the mission of the children is to pay close attention, in order to react correctly if the corresponding number has been announced. The coaches can make it harder by whispering a number or even by hiding within a sentence, i.e. ('You are doing this wrong ONE more time' and over and over again or 'We are going to do this another thirtyTWO-times') or included in an arithmetic problem. Additionally, false commands can be given: 'LET'S GO' or 'THREE!'. Over time, the children can stand back to back, crouched or lying, with closed eyes – or the command is replaced by a roshambo. ("Schnick, Schnack Schnuck")

This game is ideal for getting started in a group, as a warm up, to make the children lively or as a method to burn off extra energy!

Zigzag throwing

- Size of the group: 4+
- Materials:
  balls

This can be used as a warm-up, a concentration exercise or as a "get to meet each other" game. The children stand in a circle, a ball is provided and it must be thrown to another child. This child will then forward it again to the next child and so on, until everyone had the ball once.

初心

Everyone has to remember who the ball came from and who they forwarded it to. The final one in the circle will throw it back to the first one (make sure, that really nobody had been forgotten!), then he or she will throw it to the one who had been chosen at the first throw, and then throws repeat themselves EXACTLY in the same manner.

After a while, a second, third and fourth ball will come into play. Then the game can be played backwards – which means, from who the ball came from at first, will now become the target.

The game can be made even more difficult by either lying on the back, by lying face-up, by sitting or by running wild across the hall. Alternatively other things can be thrown as well, i.e. frisbee, garden-hose, etc.

Stick swapping

- Size of the group: 2+
- Materials:
  Sticks, shinai, bokken or something similar

One stick each is issued to all children (it should reach their hips, better if even higher), alternatively shinai, bokken or something comparable to whatever is available in the hall.

These sticks will now be placed on the floor, all children stand face to face and they will swap their places by command. The sticks remain where they are and may not tumble.

After that, the distance of both sticks will be increased, so that the swap will be more difficult. If it worked well in a group of two, it can be repeated in a group of four (all grab the stick of their partner to the right, respectively to the left) and even in a collective group with up to 30 participants, it should not cause a problem, provided that all of them concentrate.

Stick catching

- Size of the group: 2+
- Materials:
  sticks, shinai, bokken or something similar

At this exercise, the sticks are held vertically in front of the body, then let go and caught again, until they hit the floor.

To make it more complicated, the stick is let go, the chest is patted once by the hand and then the stick has to be caught again. It's even possible to pat the chest twice if the stick had been slightly thrown in the air instead of just let it go.

The same exercise can be executed with partners. One lets it go, the other has to catch. The sticks can also be thrown to one another, at best, two at once, so that a higher level of attention is necessary.

Partner guiding + robot, blind course

- Size of the group: 2+
- Materials:
  None

Most children are already familiar with guiding a partner blindly. One child needs to close his eyes or us a blindfold, the other one is the guide. Obstacles in the hall, like a complicated course or an annoying noise, can make the exercise more difficult. Also the guide can accelerate his or her speed.

A good way to upgrade the value of the game is to include the option of a robot-game: The person, who is the guide, takes the partner not by his hand but is positioned in front of him. By tapping on his head, the robot starts to walk and by tapping again, the robot stops. The robot is able to turn to other directions, provided he is in the standing position – during the whole exercise not a word is spoken. In that way the tactile security of the guide, as having somebody to cling to, is dropped.

To complicate the issue, the guide can have a number of robots – if there are more than four, it may become difficult to keep track and it may take too long to play as everyone in the group is supposed to be the guide at least once. But until this point it will be highly interesting to watch!

Additionally, a course can be built up in the hall, where designated duties need to be performed. The task of the guide is not limited to guiding the partner in a safe way through the hall, but to also provide assistance to him in order to correctly perform the assigned duties.

Task examples :

- Cones are spread zigzagged throughout the hall.
- Various types of underlay (mats, soft mats, cones, sticks or a bench turned upside down).
- Tunnels (many halls are equipped with corresponding pipes).

- Vaulting boxes that need to be climbed over.
- Ropes hung from the gym. The guide leaves his partner next to the rope so he can find his own way along it.
- A bowling game in the hall: The guided one may not continue to proceed until all cones have fallen – of course, blind and with the support of one single ball.
- Somersault or roll backwards on a mat.
- Crossing of a trampoline.
- Skateboards for crossing a certain distance.

Gun barrel

- Size of the group: 10+
- Materials:
  None

Here is the issue, a test of courage and to vividly and imaginarily experience fear. One child receives a blindfold (or closes his eyes), the others form a gun barrel in two rows next to a wall, from where the "blind" person will be shot out. The child stands with his back to the wall and then runs through the lane in the quickest possible way. In order to keep orientation, the ones who are standing around make a light sound – like a humming.

After leaving the gun barrel, the child should continue running full speed until the coach says "Stop". Even then, he does not have to stop immediately as there will still be enough space between the child and the wall on the other side. If there is a need, the coach assists with catching the running child.

The general idea of this game: The children in the gun barrel are taking responsibility for the running one, who needs to rely on them – by having eyes closed, the experience is that the hall will suddenly feel much smaller and narrower, than it actually is in reality.

The feeling that the wall is already approaching, although it is actually still far off : this feeling is fear.

Afterwards, this can be greatly evaluated by conversation, with the assessment of positive and negative aspects, of the importance of trust.

Falling down from the box

- Size of the group: 12+
- Materials:
  vaulting boxes, mats

This game is also a mixture of a test of courage and trust – with the clear message: If I have people who I can trust, I am able to achieve more than if I had to do it all by myself.

At "Falling down from the box", a child will fall down to the front from a vaulting box, stiff as a board. The other children are standing in double rows in front of the vaulting box in order to catch the falling one.

In order to save the joints and bones of the children who are trying to catch, they will not hold their hands out, but stand with their arms casually on both sides. The coach will then give the command to the child who is going to drop down: "One, two, three"– at "three" he will drop down. Then the coach will give the command "Happ!" – that will be the moment when the children will raise their arms in order to catch the falling child.

What is hereby important: The arms hang casually left and right, and at the command "Happ" all children will raise their arms by an angle of 90 degrees. The upper arms remain hung, only the forearm will be bent. This is really important, as in this way the shoulder muscles do not need to operate, only the muscles of biceps and triceps.

初心

The children who catch have to contribute their part too – if someone does not show enough effort, it will easily be apparent. The falling child truly has to have the courage in remaining as stiff as a board – otherwise the others who are standing on the bottom will hardly be able to catch. As part of the test of courage it is ok to admit to being afraid – in this case. An alternative method is for a child to lay on the floor between the legs of the ones who are trying to catch. This is also dangerous and exciting, but allows for those who are afraid of heights.

It is very important to pay attention to the space between the children who are trying to catch: A large number of them should have the capability to catch simultaneously and the double rows should stand neither too near nor too far from each other in order to guarantee an optimal catch.

This game needs to be carefully prepared by the coaches. The children first need to practice with a partner, who catches them from falling backwards (most of them may already have experienced this as it is often performed in a trust exercise), then fall backwards onto a soft mat, from there so the height can be adjusted or raised with vaulting boxes.

Falling into the arms of the other children is the highlight in a sequence of exercises – which serves well in recognizing that to cope with fear it can be handled in a step by step and gentle approach, instead of starting an exercise by knowing it is too difficult to begin with.

Assembly line

- Size of the group: 10+
- Materials:
  None

This is a great way to practice body tension, teamwork and solidarity within a group: The children lie on their backs in a row next to each other, but by the zipper principle. Between the heads of two children there will be a third and the legs are pointing in the other direction, so that all the heads of the group are forming a straight line.

The children now stretch their arms upwards and the coaches place one child at a time onto the up-stretched arms. The child is stiff as a statue and therefore can be carried onto the other side, where he is caught by another coach and put back on his feet.

This exercise only works well if all work together: The one, who has to be carried, has to remain stiff as a statue and the rest of the group has to contribute their part to be successful. Sometimes it is a waiting game, especially in bigger groups.

Practices on soft mats

- Size of the group: 10+
- Materials:
  soft mats

A variety of cooperation games and practices are achievable with the usage of available soft-mats. Among children, mat-surfing is very popular, where the soft mats are placed on the floor with the slippery side faced down. The children are divided into teams, who then push the mat to the wall across the hall. With the kids jumping onto the mat altogether, the mat slides forward with momentum and gives the impression that they are 'surfing'. This requires co-operation and attention so no one jumps behind the mat or onto other 'surfers'.

Also a very nice practice is the mat-balance, where a soft mat is placed onto its side-edges between two vaulting boxes. The children stabilize the mat, while one child balances over the narrow side on top of the mat. Good cushioning is important, as many children are going to plunge – due to the fact, that most mats are simply unstable.

The children will experience a plunge on purpose, by knocking over the mats: Thereby, a soft mat is leaned against the wall and is tightly held by the other children, while one climbs up the mat and is trying to sit on the narrow side on top. By command, the mat will plunge to the front onto cushioning, which had been placed there in order to avoid injuries. This plunge is a test of courage and therefore also calm behavior is required. In case the one who is plunging does not act carefully enough, it will plunge backwards and instead of landing on his feet, he will land on his back like a turtle.

Candy belt

- Size of the group: 4+
- Materials:
  belts

This game will only work in martial arts, where a belt is worn: All children stick the ends of their belts into the actual belt, in this way

two "candies" are created – ribbons, which can be pulled out by the others.

Now, two partners at a time can always get together. The mission is to pull off both "candies", (both ribbons) from the belt of their counterpart. The one, who is in the possession of two hanging belt ends will be punished by, i.e. sit-ups, but after that, he can stick the ends of the belts back again.

The game can be played by a group of three or by a group of four – or simply, everyone against everyone. In this case not only peripheral vision is trained, but also cleverness.

Carrot pulling

- Size of the group: 7+
- Materials:
  None

This game is easy to play and is a lot of fun. It fits well in between short training breaks. It has to do with solidarity and how to take care of one another – but it is also a question of how to gain acceptance and how to get to the bottom of opportunities to do that.

The children lay down in a big circle and grab each other by the hands or forearms. The mission is to cling to one another, so that a little group (or a single individual) of carrot-pullers fail to pull individual children out of the group.

Anyone who gets pulled out of the group, will become a carrot-puller himself. That happens, as soon as ANY contact with the other carrots has been lost.

The mission of the carrot-puller is to cut back the solidarity of the carrots. That can be easily regulated – i.e. the children are only allowed to touch the legs of the carrots – or as an exercise on the subject of violence with the rule: "anything goes, but don't let anybody get hurt".

"Being hurt" is defined as anything that physically or mentally hurts someone. That complicates the matter, as most of the carrots are sensitive in different ways. In general, ideas are very, very versatile, like tickling something out of somebody or pulling their trousers, etc.

The coaches need to work on these basic rules as soon as the situation turns out to become a nasty one.

Cone stealing

- Size of the group: 10+
- Materials:
  soft mats, cones

This game is all about fighting: A stack of cones is built up right in the center of the hall, one soft mat on each side. Two teams are formed by the children.

After the starting signal, the aim of the game is for each team to collect as many cones as possible – and place them under their own soft mat. It is also important for a team to successfully defend their own cones under the soft mat, as it is allowed to steal them from there.

Basically here is the rule: Anything goes, but don't let anybody hurt. It is defined exactly in the way to match the content in the chapter "prevention of violence": Mental injuries count.

This game requires a great level of attention from the coaches in order to let the game proceed without stress, as the children are ambitious and not everyone is equally sensitive and tough enough. Additionally, after a short while, some tend to forget about the cones but rather stay involved with single conflicts. On top of that, the children are armed with cones. All of that requires a lot of discipline within the tumult.

Ideally, during the game, the children are going to discover opportunities for co-operation: Passing the cones ("passing game"), securing the cone-carrier and protecting their own mat.

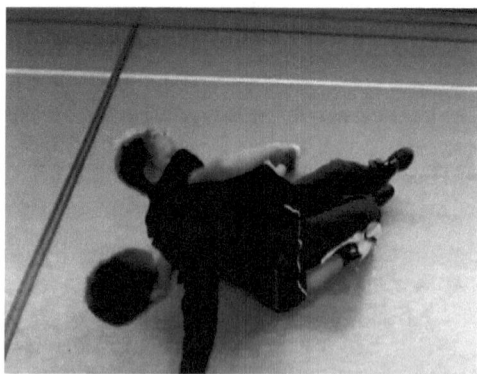

Another variation of the game is to place the cones under soft mats on both edges of the hall, instead of right in the center and each team is provided with a vaulting box. In that way, the cones, which have

reached the box are "safe" – that shortens the length of the game and decreases the fight-intensity at both ends of the hall.

Sumo Wrestling

- Size of the group: 4+
- Materials:
  gymnastics mats

Sumo wrestlers are leaving a 'heavy' impression behind for children, and therefore their sport suits a "trimmed" version as a fighting game for the training of martial arts.

The rules are thereby quite easy: Both opponents may only touch the floor with the bottom of their feet and may not leave the mats. Other than that, anything goes, but also nobody may get hurt.

The ones who are not in a competition just yet, are responsible for controlling the mats and making sure that they will not slide apart.

The fight starts with both fighters positioned on two opposite sides of the mat field, bent at their waist with their hands on the floor. After the referees' starting command, both hands are raised.

For the performance, a "Japanese tournament" is recommended: The children are seated in a circle around the mats. The competition winner always remains on the mat, the loser returns into the circle and makes way for the next challenger. In this way, the good fighters are very active, but on the other hand also exhausted after a while.

For analysis it is recommended to take a very close look at how the individual competitors actually achieved their victory. Methods of intimidation work well at sumo – someone who is approaching the mat expressing a confidence of victory to his opponent has got a good chance of succeeding.

The game can become very wild and it's important for opponents to realize that it may be necessary to concede sometimes. If desired, these issues can be trained by preliminary exercises before the actual sumo-wrestling competition.

Chinese dragon

- Size of the group: 7+
- Materials:
  None

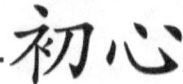

In this exercise, co-operation and fighting skills are equally in demand, which can be explained well by telling the children that for the Chinese there is no difference between "dragon" and "snake". And this is what it is about – the children initially are going to form a snake.

For that, they are lined up in one row, just like doing the conga at a party (this explanation is understood by most). However hands cannot be put on the shoulder of the person in front, as all will immediately start to move quickly and intensively. And this could lead to strangulation marks on the neck.

The children must grab each other at the hips – or in certain kinds of sports, if possible, grab each other at the belt. That is the best solution by far.

The formed snake can only be defeated by two ways: Either by tearing one child out of the snake or if at least one child lets go of the person in front. Alternatively if someone gets hold of the snakes' tail – in other words: If a catcher touches the LAST ONE of the snake.

初心

The mission of the whole group is to protect the last one at the end of the snake – but at the same time keeping aware to make sure the row does not tear.

But who is the one that catches? The foremost child of the snake is released and takes a step forward. Then he turns around – and becomes the catcher. This will remain until the catcher has touched the last one or if the snake is torn. If the catcher is successful, he will now become the end of the snake and the next child becomes the catcher.

If the group solves the task well, it is almost impossible for the catcher to be successful. Which means: The whole group is always standing between the catcher and the end of the snake. For that, all participants need to pay close attention, react quickly and may not let go from the person in front. If the catcher had been unsuccessful with his attempts, the coach is able to intervene and declare the group as the victors – including praise because this game only works well with excellent co-operation from all.

In reference to the size of the groups: With more than 10 children in a group, it will not work. So, if there are too many children, it is recommended to form two snakes, or even three or four. The fact that these can run into one another, and that the children will have to be aware of their own catcher, their own team-mates and also the other snakes in the hall, does not hurt – it even increases the level of excitement.

Medicine ball rugby

- Size of the group: 10+
- Materials:
  medicine ball, two mats

This is another fighting game with a high level fun factor: One mat each is distributed to two teams. The mats represent the goals and are situated near the wall at the end of the hall. The medicine ball will be placed in the center of the hall.

After the game has begun, the mission is to bring the ball onto the mat of the other team. Ball and player have to arrive at the same time in order to obtain a point. Throwing the ball is prohibited and the players have to fight their way in order to actually land on the mat.

This game also can be played with more than a single ball, but it requires closer supervision from the coaches – rugby quickly becomes pretty rough.

Alternatively, the game also can be played without mats, but instead with many more balls: At the beginning they will all be placed in the center of the hall. After the game has begun, the teams have to put the highest possible number of balls in their opponents field. At the final whistle, the team with the least balls wins.

Clothes pins robbery

- Size of the group: 8+
- Materials:
  plenty of clothes pins

This game is ideal for warming-up. One clothes pin (optionally two or three) is distributed to each child and attached on some spot of their clothes. Now the fight starts: Who gathers the most clothes pins wins.

As a possible second half twist of the game, it can be turned the other way around and those in possession of the LEAST number of clothes pins, by attaching them onto their opponents' clothes, wins.

This game can also be performed very well within belt-wearing martial arts and use these belts for the game: The winner is the one who gets hold of the most belts. However the fight could become pretty rough, as a belt is not easy to be caught.

Cowboy

- Size of the group: 9+
- Materials:
  mats

Two children are named to become cowboys, the others are 'wild horses'. The cowboys will receive a 'stall' (optionally several stalls), represented by mats which are placed on the floor. Their job now is to catch individual horses and bring them into their stable.

They will certainly offer resistance. Nevertheless, if the cowboys are able to bring a horse into the stable, this horse will change itself into a cowboy and will assist the others by catching another horse.

This game is a rustic alternative of the popular "chain catching" – but there is more of a fight involved, which certainly accommodates to the nature of martial arts training.

Trolls and Fairies

- Size of the group: 10+
- Materials:
  None

Similar to 'cowboy', this game is also a 'catching game'. The children change themselves in to fairies, and then run across the hall. But a few of them are trolls. The job of the trolls is to catch the fairies.

If a fairy is touched, it will change into a tree: He or she has to stand still in a cowgirl position, with their arms stretched up.

The other fairies can change them back from a tree to a fairy, by crawling through their legs. An important note for the children: Crawling or sliding through the legs of a boy is supposed to be done from the back. From the front, a quick approach can involve painful consequences!

Co-operation and special attention to who is in the need of support is required for both, trolls and fairies. The game is a lot of fun and easy to be explained – it is a great game for warming-up or for a finish.

Circle wrestling / Mats restling

- Size of the group: 8+
- Materials:
  mats (if available)

Optionally playable on a soft mat or on a field of mats, which need to be spread out – an even easier use is the center circle of the gym (sports hall). However, there is quite a danger of painful falls.

The task of the game is for all children to be located in the named field. The aim is to push down the others while remaining on the mat or within the circle.

This is a fast moving, but most of all, quite a challenging game where assertiveness as well as consideration can be trained.

This practice works especially well with spread out judo mats.

Wrestling practices: Rising, turning

- Size of the group: 2+
- Materials:
  mats (if available)

This is a pretty simple exercise, which requires a lot of fighting effort. A child lies on the floor and a partner lays across on top. The child that lies under has the desire to get up, but the partner is trying to prevent this. As an alternative, it can be reversed, so that the partner, who lies on top, is trying to avoid being turned over.

It will be even harder, if the child that lies down has more than one opponent to fight– with four opponents getting up is almost impossible.

Zombie or Dragon's tail

- Size of the group: 8+
- Materials:
  ball (if available)

Most children may have already heard of the game 'Zombie', therefore in order to avoid any upcoming conflicts with the rules details have to be clarified with the children up front. Basically it is fairly simple: All children run across the hall. There is a single or multiple balls, and the person who gets hit by the ball is out and must sit on the bench.

The ones who have to sit on the bench can go back into the game, providing the person who has hit them is then hit himself. This certainly requires an enormous amount of attention: As the children not only have to notice when they are hit, but also by whom. Otherwise they are out of the game and can no longer return.

Alternatively the game can be played without balls, but with belts instead. It will be more complicated as there are not a clear lydefined number of balls in the game and also due to the fact that anyone can hit anyone. Before the game starts, it needs to be agreed which target zone is an absolutely no-no. This is a helpful practice in order to recognize and sensitive specify parts of the body which are out of bounds.

初心

Rope footrace

- Size of the group: 10+
- Materials:
  one rope

Concentration and courage are required for this practice. But also a recognition of ones own limits in a timely manner in order to minimize risks.

The children must have a good ability of counting – therefore this practice is only appropriate to a limited extent for the most little ones.

Firstly, two equally sized groups are formed. Each group assigns a number to the children in the group so there is a "1", a "2", a "3" and so on.

A coach is stands in the center and holds a rope in the air. Next, a number, equivalent to a command, will be announced. Both children, who are assigned by this number in their group start running – the winner is the one who arrives at the rope first. The one who arrives too late is out of the game and has to take a seat on the bench. His assigned number is forwarded to another member of their own team. This person will now have to react when his assigned number or the additional number of the eliminated team-member is called.

That requires concentration, because the more players are eliminated, the more numbers have to be remembered. Simultaneously, they will have to start running and also need to decide on how much risk to take in order to avoid a crash into the opponent of the other team who is also sprinting to the rope.

American Gladiators

- Size of the group: 2+
- Materials:
  one bench, mats, fighting equipment (if available)

This game has to do with balance and co-ordination as well as martial arts and courage. It takes place on an upside down bench which has been put onto a soft mat. Additional mats should also be placed around this fighting field in order to cushion somebody's fall.

Both players meet in the middle of the bench, their job is to push the other opponent off the bench.

Additional rules can be added to this task: Both players take themselves by their hands and have to get the other one off the bench, either by pulling or by pushing. Both players have to grab each other at the back. Another option is they have to fight with a swimming noodle (woggle), which is provided to them.

A great fighting practice with a lot of fun!

Marbles hunting

- Size of the group: 8+
- Materials:
  marbles, two vaulting boxes

Similar to miscellaneous games with cones, the point is also to put the highest number of marbles onto a vaulting box that has been turned upside down. Two teams play against each other. Every team has got one box turned upside down which serves as their marble storage. At the beginning all the marbles will be placed in the center of the hall.

In comparison to other games with cones, this game is definitely more quieter, as the marbles may only be touched by the children's feet. They must try to get a hold of them only with their toes.

This is not easy –especially as the muscular system of the feet is often insufficiently skilled, because nowadays shoes are equipped with arch supports.

Chain catching

- Size of the group: 10+
- Materials:
  None

This game belongs in the repertoire of any sports coach and can be played in two ways: With a chain of children that is constantly growing or by splitting this chain of 8 into a number of 4 chains with 2 children or respectively into 2 chains with 4 children each.

We have found the best experience is with a chain that is constantly growing as the issue of co-operation becomes considerably obvious.

Short summary: Two children begin as the ones that need to catch. They hold their hands and must not loose one another. If they successfully are able to catch a child, this child will join the chain. Only both ends of the chain have the ability to catch, the others in the chain can only stick together and assist in surrounding the child who needs to be caught.

Island game

- Size of the group: 8+
- Materials:
  big case, small boxes
  mats for cushioning, ropes

This game works only in gymnastic halls equipped with ropes that hang down from the ceiling and where children can swing (we are talking about the ropes which usually are tagged with the advice to avoid making any knots in the ropes besides the existing integrated knots).

The ropes will be stretched out to meet a high case. During the game, children will swing down from there and land on a small island, which is represented by small boxes. This island is surrounded by mats, which represent the sea. If one child accidentally touches the sea, the whole group has lost and has to start all over again.

The children's task is it to swing down from the high case, one after another, in the way so all of them find a space on the island. If this works fine, the coaches can shrink the size of the island by removing some of the small boxes until the task truly becomes a challenge.

Children become quite inventive; they climb on top of each other, build pyramids or even find other alternative ways. A disappointing experience of failure during the game, which may happen after a while (due to the fact,that it is no longer achievable because of the inadequate size of the island or amount of boxes), requires the coaches to skillfully cheer up the defeated ones.

Balancing act

- Size of the group: 8+
- Materials:
  a bench, that is turned upside down

This is an excellent concentration practice: The children are lined up on an upside down bench. The point of this exercise is for the child who stands the furthest left to make his way through the line of children until he arrives at the other end of the bench, but taking care not to make anyone tumble. This is a good exercise for team work and it requires good balance.

As an option, the children on the bench also can be sorted by age, alphabetically by their first names, by the size of their shoes, by the number of their brothers and sisters and so on. But, to make it more difficult, this needs to happen without a word being spoken.

Hole in the floor

- Size of the group: 2+
- Materials:
  hoops

A single hoop is distributed to two children. It will be placed on the floor between these two individuals. The loop represents a deep hole, where certainly nobody wants to fall into.

The task is to find a way to pull the opponent into this hole. This is a standing game which generally proceeds in a fairly controlled manner.

Silent mail

- Size of the group: 14+
- Materials:
  two benches

A game of co-operation, which trains cognitive ability and requires concentration: Both benches stand parallel to each other. The children are separated into two groups then sit astride a bench with their eyes closed.

The child on the very end of the bench may turn around and open his eyes. The task of this child is it to gather items which are given by the coach. The coach holds up two items. Item 1 is forwarded by tapping on the right shoulder, item 2 by tapping on the left shoulder. The children who have their eyes closed must forward the items in the quickest way possible to the child who is sitting at the very front of the bench. When the child at the front has the item he has to shout out either 'item 1' or 'item 2'. The team who shout the correct number first, scores a point. Then the child from the front rotates to the end and the game starts again.

Flood

- Size of the group: 8+
- Materials:
  several hoops

This game is similar to the popular "Travel to Jerusalem" game. The children run across the hall and on a specific command the hall will be flooded with high water and all have to rescue themselves by reaching the hoops in the quickest time possible.

There are two options available for the period of time for the children to reach dry land: Either the coach counts backwards "Three – Two – One – Zero" – and whoever is not in a hoop by the call of "Zero" is out of the game. Or the last two children who have not reached a hoop yet are out and have to sit on the bench.

As an aggravating option individual hoops can be removed – or the coach throws the hoops on the floor after announcing his command. Throwing hoops can even be the actual signal.

Other optional signals can be making a specific gesture which means the children have to concentrate or telling a story with certain keywords which mean hoops have to be found immediately. The story can include several colors with the children having to rescue themselves into the hoop with the corresponding color.

Monster legs

- Size of the group: 8+
- Materials:
  None

The children have to form a monster in this game. This monster has only got a certain number of legs – and this number matches the number of limbs of which the children are allowed to touch the floor.

The task can be that the monster has to leave the room with a specified "x" number of legs. Then the children need to think about how it is manageable to touch the floor with only this certain number of arms and legs.

Or the issue can be to run across the hall and form such a monster if the command is announced.

Another alternative is for the children to run across the hall and the coach calls out two numbers: The first number indicates the number of children per monster; the second number represents the number of legs that can touch the floor. That causes even more of a rush and is a lot of fun.

Pyramids constructor

- Size of the group: 8+
- Materials:
  soft mats

This is a relaxing game without any special requirements, which can be played well as a foot race: A soft mat is provided to each group of children, which symbolizes a stone that needs to be brought from the stone pit to the construction site. The stone is certainly too heavy to be pushed, therefore ideally it should be rolled. But there are no wheels available.

The basic aim is for the children to lift the mat in coordination with each another, knock it over, pick it up again and so on. That causes a lot of noise, a lot of fun and works quite well in competition with other groups. Due to the fact, that this game is so simple, it can be easily used as relaxation after a concentrated training phase.

Put the stick down on the floor

- Size of the group: 8+
- Materials:
  one long stick or pole

The number of children participating in this game should be a minimum of 8 and a maximum of 12. They are all supposed to work with a stick (or pole). The pole must not be too heavy, as it is laid onto the children's outstretched index fingers.

The task is to lay down the stick at a slow pace and in conjunction with each other. There is only one condition: All 16 index fingers need to touch the stick at all times.

The co-ordination between the children is difficult – experience shows, that despite all efforts, the stick usually moves upwards. This exercise also works well with adults.

Getting up together

- Size of the group: 2+
- Materials:
  None

A simple, small exercise: two children sit on the floor, back to back, arm in arm, the legs stretched out. They then get up together and without letting go of other one. That requires a lot more body tension and co-ordination than firstly assumed.

One version of this game is for the children to stand front facing each other, feet placed against each other and holding each others hand. Now they lean backwards with stretched arms, so that they are held by the weight of the partner. On a rotating basis the two individuals, linked with each other, try to get onto their knees. The mission of the partner is to balance the movement.

初心

Example lessons:

Exemplary concepts of lessons to start your own Bonsai group

初心

初心

The following example lessons describe the start of a Bonsai group as it can run successfully in karate. The individual lessons are built-up in the way to match a growing number of participants – we anticipate a low number of participation at the beginning, but this number may increase with every new hour.

Additional comments on how to associate with parents as well as details of general conditions are also included.

With these lessons we are basically trying to provide suggestions to you. Every dojo has its very own requirements, each coach his own approach. Based on our experience it is beneficial and important to prepare lessons in advance – however, a good coach owns the ability of a "threshold educationalist" and evaluates the group when entering the room ("at the threshold") and accordingly matches his concept.

Experience, creativity and self-assurance are thereby required. We hope that these example lessons will assist you in obtaining these necessary qualities.

初心

Lesson 1

                                            60 minutes
                         Size of the group: 10+

Materials:
One hula hoop per child and one soft ball

Greeting (5 min)

- Coaches and children greet each other in a traditional way. Don´t underestimate the effect that a full-blown ritual in this moment already has.
- Introduction of the present coaches (and, if applicable, also assistant coaches)
- Short preview of the upcoming hour

Question time (5 min)

- What actually is... (karate, judo etc.)...?
- Where do martial arts come from?
- What is it all about?
- (The children will certainly tell about the training to their circle of friends and acquaintances and therefore this information is worth its weight in gold)

Dog house (10 min)

- A child has the task of being a 'catcher'. Children who have been caught by the catcher have to stand with legs apart, right at the spot where they have been caught, and cannot return to the game until another child has crawled through their legs. While doing so, the catcher can not catch both children. (this is a version of 'Trolls and Fairies')
- Alternatively: Octopus hunting.
The caught participant has to sit on the floor, making him a stationary 'octopus' and continue his catch from there. Whoever is left at the end becomes the new catcher.

The first techniques (15 min)

- Techniques in a circle.
  All participants and coaches stand together in a circle. First basic techniques will be shown in order to immediately join.
- The coach tells a small story, that 'describes' the individual motion. So, a snatched step forward is becoming a step into the imaginary mouth of a huge toad with big teeth. The leg may not drag over the floor, as it has to be stepped INTO the mouth and not against from bottom up. The necessary snap back of the forward leg is natural, otherwise the monster bites and the leg is gone. It is quite obvious, isn't it?
- Such or a similar graphic descriptions, close to the imagination of the children, should be elaborated in advance for all relevant techniques:
- Hitting- and pushing techniques
- Kicks
- Blocking and defense techniques

Battleships (15 min)

- All children are equipped with a hula hoop and run around the hall. The 'ship reamer', with the ability to sink the ships has to throw a ball into the hoop of the "ships" to make them sink. The "sunken ships" have to put their hoop on the floor and need to stand still in the hoop. Another "ship" is able to "rescue sunken ships" by putting its hoop over the participant in the hoop. In this way the "sunken ship" is rescued and can go back into the game.
- Alternative:
  The ship can only be rescued if another ship's commander also steps into the hoop. Now there are 2 children with 2 hoops on its way. If they have been sunk again, they need another child to rescue them. A maximum number of four children with their four hoops can play together. If they are hit one more time, they have to drop out of the game.

Good bye (10 min)

- Traditional Good bye, depending on the martial arts
- Short summary of the experiences of the past hour! 'This is what you are already able to achieve ...!'
- A short outlook to the next lesson.

Notes about the parents:

Here you should not be left to your own resources. Working with several coaches you can make sure that from time to time at least one of them gets in touch with the parents to provide explanations or provide answers to their questions.

Thereby, the following issues should be addressed:

- Who is the POC (point of contact) in case of any questions, problems and complaints arise?
- What does the organizational progress of a training-lesson look like?
- Which topics are covered in the training?
- May parents always be spectators?
- How long does the "taster time" last?
- Point to further lessons or offers of the club or the school.

It should also be addressed to the parents that they are only spectators during the lessons and that they do not carry any responsibilities – and in the following lessons it is also important to point out that by the continuing progress of the lessons and familiarization of the children to the new environment, they may become a disrupting factor. To express this in a diplomatic way may be a real challenge!

Food and drink on the bench, as well as noisy talking, are not permitted from the start.

Besides any conversation, it is important that something is provided to the parents where the name of the club, the school and the coach are listed, as well as the POC (Point of Contact) in case of any questions, problems or complaints arising. But under no circumstances should it be the application form or a listing of charges. These questions are not part of the training!

初心

What do the parents need?

In general, children adjust to a new environment and new people around them quite quickly. That may be because for children *everything* is new anyway, whether it is the kindergarten, school or now the trial lesson in the martial arts club.

For the parents it is a different story - new environments, different parents, young coaches and the desire to do the very best for their own child. It is not surprising that many parents appear at training with an amount of fear – i.e. worries that their child does not get along or that it may not show the same good performance as other children. This is often expressed by statements like: "My child has only got an impaired amount of motoric skills" and "I am not sure, if he can make it or not!"

A good coach is able to remove the fear of the parents. Listening to their worries and then giving them assurance that you are taking care of every individual child are of a great help.

It can also be helpful to shake hands with the attending parents before the lesson starts. Thereby it is important that the coach approaches the parents in a way that it will become a natural act. In this way, new parents have the opportunity of an easier way of getting started and eventually can also bring up personal matters.

Lesson 2

> 60 minutes
> Size of the group: 15+
>
> *Materials*
> No specific

Greeting (5 min)

- Coaches and children greet each other traditionally.
- Introduction for the new participants.
  (From experience, bonsai groups grow heavily in the first few lessons, including a significant fluctuation).
- Short preview of the upcoming hour.

Question time (5 min)

- What actually is... (Karate, Judo etc.)...?
- Where do martial arts come from?
- And it was invented by whom?
- (Some of the children may already have some answers ready from the first lesson).

Pair running (10 min)

- Two children have to run side by side, one of them is the leader, the other one needs to be orientated by the leader.
- Variation: The follower needs to keep track of either the right or the left shoulder of the leader. Wild twists and turns will make it hard for the other. Also, the shoulder can suddenly be changed if such a command is given by the coach.
- The follower has to imitate the leader's movements. The creativity is unlimited.
- The follower constantly has to circle around the leader, but this is definitely not easy, caused by impaired motor skills.

Pushing and pulling (10 min)

- Two children get together to form a team. The children stand across from each other and hold hands. On the command 'push', all of the children have to try to push away their training partner. On the command 'pull', all of the children have to try pulling each other out of balance.
- Consequently, discuss the basic position.
    - What does the proper position look like?
    - For what reason is a certain position particularly advantageous for pushing or pulling?
- After this explanation and with their just obtained knowledge, the children should get another opportunity for a round of 'pushing' and 'pulling'.
- This practice creates the basic position for this level (-> lesson 3).

The first techniques (10 min)

- Techniques in a circle.
  Once again, all children stand together in a circle and repeat the techniques of the previous lesson:
- Hitting- and pushing techniques
- Kicks
- Blocking and defense techniques

Jump over (10 min)

- The children split up equally in the hall and sit on the floor with outstretched legs. One child tries to catch another child.
- If the haunted one runs out of steam, he just jumps over the legs of a seated child, which then consequently will try to haunt the previous catcher.
- The previous runner can sit down on the floor with tucked up legs.

Good bye (10 min)

- Traditional Good bye, depending on the martial art style
- Short summary of the experiences in the past hour!
  'This is what you are already able to achieve ...!'
- A short outlook to the next lesson.

Lesson 3

60 minutes
Size of the group: 20+

Materials:
One skipping rope for two children each

Greeting (5 min)
- Coaches and children greet each other traditionally.
- Short preview of the upcoming hour.

Question time (5 min)
- Here is where the children, who already attended the first lessons, can get involved – they can tell the newcomers about their experiences in the class, what it is all about and what exactly is going on.

Foot race of the animals! (5 min)
- The children's task is it to cross the hall in the fastest possible way. They need to imitate animal sounds, which are provided by the coach. For example: 'Frog'- thereby the children have to cross the hall, croaking like frogs.
- Following the previous hour, where the children had to deal with the pushing and pulling of training partners, now the task can be to imagine how it feels to push or pull a heavy object. Later on, you can return once again to this idea of the basic position.

Horse racing (10 min)
- Two children each get together to form a team, one skipping rope is provided to each team. One child puts the skipping rope around the hip of the other child. The "horse" now needs to try to cross the hall in the fastest possible way and the 'horse guide' may put up some resistance. Once the teams crossed the hall, it will be changed to the other way around.
- ATTENTION: The skipping ropes may not be wrapped around the hands, as in case of emergency it cannot be released fast enough. Also the children may not simply release or suddenly pull the rope. This practice also leads back to the basic position.

Techniques (10 min)

- All children repeat the techniques in the circle. The coaches shall hold on to the 'technique-stories' – for one thing for the participants, for another thing in order to embed it as general knowledge. Based on experience, even after many years children still remember it.
- Hitting- and pushing techniques
- Kicks
- Blocking and defense techniques

'Paramedics ball' (10 min)

- Two teams of the same size are formed and lined up on both sides of the wall, divided by the center line. A mat is placed at both ends of the hall. The children are supposed to throw off the children of the other team. If a child has been hit, he has to lie on the floor and may no longer move. The other participants of their team have to carry the "wounded" to the mat (into the hospital). While the "wounded" are carried, the helping children may not be thrown off.
- It is a matter of teamwork and the point is to take care of each other and to stick together.

Good bye (10 min)

- Traditional Good bye, depending on the martial arts style
- Short summary of the experiences from the past hour!
- A short outlook to the next lesson.

Lesson 4

60 minutes
Size of the group: 25+

Materials:
Perhaps material for the relay

Greeting (5 min)

- Coaches and children greet each other traditionally (as in the previous lessons).
- Short review, welcoming new participants and a preview to today's hour.

Question time (5 min)

- The question time in the 4th hour can also be made into a competition. The children are divided into two groups and the group who does not know the answer or replies too slowly has to run one lap.

'Tapping' (10 min)

- Two individual children stand together. One child stands behind the other one and communicates various commands by tapping with his or her finger. These commands need to be executed into movements in the fastest possible way. The communication of commands works only by tapping with the finger.
  tap on the right arm -> raise right arm
  tap on the left arm -> raise left arm
  tap on the right leg -> lift right leg
  tap on the left leg -> lift left leg
- Optionally, certain techniques can also be repeated this way by having them combined with tapping.

Romeo and Juliet (5 min)

- At this game, two individual children play the roles of Romeo and Juliet, who want to find one another. They stand in two different corners of the hall. Their mission is to touch each other – the other children are the wicked families, who try to avoid it. An interesting running- and jostling-game, often with a surprising outcome.

Relay (5 min)

- Relays are quite multi-variant games and there is no limit for using imagination. The easiest way is to create two equal-sized teams, which have to line up on one side of the hall. Then the children of each group have to run and touch the opposite side of the hall and then return. The next team-member has to wait before running until he or she has been touched by the previous runner of his team.
- Alternatives can be formed through varying tasks – i.e. certain techniques need to be executed before the high five, specific tasks need to be performed on the course or the game must be played with closed eyes or on skate boards ...

Basic position with techniques (10 min)

- The children once again get together in a circle – a line-up that should already have a ritual feeling by now. Now the techniques will not only be performed in the standing position, but by a small step to the front or to the back. Thereby all techniques can be performed within a small radius and can be easily corrected.
- Hitting- and pushing techniques
- Kicks
- Blocking and defense techniques

'Circle wrestling / mat wrestling' (10 min)

- Optionally playable on a soft mat or on a field of spread out mats – even easier is the use of the center circle of the gym. But there is the danger of painful accidents and therefore the coaches must pay much more attention.
- The task of the game: All children are located in the mentioned field and their job is on the one hand to push down the others, but on the other hand to keep oneself on the mat, or alternatively in the circle. This is quite an emotional game with a mostly fighting touch where assertiveness and consideration can be practiced.

Good bye (10 min)

- Traditional Good bye, depending on the martial arts style
- The outlook for the next lesson including the promise of new adventures that will exceed the basic techniques.

Notes about the parents:

By no later than the 4th lesson, a large number of questions may have emerged – if not, certain issues should anyway be addressed once again.

That can occur during the training hour while the starting games are on the go. But also the end of the training is a good time when more parents are present in order to pick up their offspring.

The following points should be summarized:

- Registration
- List of charges (Application fee, annual charges, membership fee)
- Service overview (club ID card, training ID card etc.)
- Purchase order for their training suits

Finally: "The application forms and the order lists for the karate suits will be distributed to your children at the end of the lesson. In case, there are any further questions you are more than welcome to get in touch with me after the training!"

初心

初心

The authors want to thank for all the support from

... our students and fellow teachers in our
dojos in Cologne, Overath, Lindlar, Kürten, Bergisch Gladbach,

... the many participants in our "Bonsai martial arts" workshops,

... and especially Lyn Thurman
(www.rosmerta.co.uk)
for the help with translating the book into proper English.

If you want to book a training with the authors,
don´t hesitate to get in contact.
Bookings are possible via the Venture Dragon Martial Arts Clubs:

http://www.vd-kampfkunst.de

or write to the ShoShin Projekt directly:
projekt@shoshin.info

初心

www.ingramcontent.com/pod-product-compliance
Lightning Source LLC
Chambersburg PA
CBHW032028230426
43671CB00005B/242